# TREASURES
*from the*
# HEART

**Crossway books by Cheryl V. Ford**

*The Pilgrim's Progress Devotional*
*Treasures from the Heart*

WOMEN OF THE WORD

# TREASURES
*from the*
# HEART

*The Value
of Godly
Character*

# CHERYL V. FORD

CROSSWAY BOOKS • WHEATON, ILLINOIS
A DIVISION OF GOOD NEWS PUBLISHERS

Cover photo and design: Liita Forsyth

First printing 2000

Printed in the United States of America

Unless otherwise designated, Scripture is taken from the *Holy Bible: New International Version®*. Copyright © 1973, 1978, 1984 by International Bible Society. Used by permission of Zondervan Publishing House. All rights reserved.

The "NIV" and "New International Version" trademarks are registered in the United States Patent and Trademark Office by International Bible Society. Use of either trademark requires the permission of International Bible Society.

Scripture references marked KJV are taken from the King James Version.

Scripture quotations taken from the *New Revised Standard Version* are identified NRSV. Copyright © 1989 by the Division of Christian Education of the National Council of the Churches of Christ in the U.S.A. Published by Thomas Nelson, Inc. Used by permission of the National Council of the Churches of Christ in the U.S.A.

Verses marked TLB are taken from *The Living Bible* © 1971. Used by permission of Tyndale House Publishers, Inc., Wheaton, IL 60189. All rights reserved.

**Library of Congress Cataloging-in-Publication Data**
Ford, Cheryl V.
   Treasures from the heart : the value of godly character / Cheryl V. Ford.
      p.  cm.— (Women of the Word)
   ISBN 1-58134-202-0 (alk. paper)
   1. Women in the Bible—Biography.  2. Christian women—Religious life.
I. Title.
BS575.F67  2000
220.9'2—dc21
                                                            00-009445
                                                            CIP

| 15 | 14 | 13 | 12 | 11 | 10 | 09 | 08 | 07 | 06 | 05 | 04 | 03 | 02 | 01 | 00 |
|----|----|----|----|----|----|----|----|----|----|----|----|----|----|----|----|
| 15 | 14 | 13 | 12 | 11 | 10 | 9  | 8  | 7  | 6  | 5  | 4  | 3  | 2  | 1  |    |

# Contents

PREFACE TO THE SERIES     7

ACKNOWLEDGMENTS     11

INTRODUCTION     13

1. MARY MAGDALENE: The Yielded Heart     17

2. JEZEBEL: The Controlling Heart     31

3. RAHAB: The Discerning Heart     45

4. EVE: The Seducible Heart     61

5. RUTH: The Flexible Heart     77

6. MICHAL: The Hardened Heart     93

7. SARAH (Sarai): The Faithful Heart     109

8. POTIPHAR'S WIFE: The Unfaithful Heart     125

9. MARY OF BETHANY: The Undivided Heart     139

10. LOT'S WIFE: The Divided Heart     155

11. ABIGAIL: The Prudent Heart     175

12. DELILAH: The Manipulative Heart     191

NOTES     206

# PREFACE TO THE SERIES

This series is for women who want to see genuine spiritual awakening in their own lives and homes, in their churches, and in their nation. We hear dramatic reports from around the world of things God is doing. We see stirrings in our nation, too; but we desperately need more than faint stirrings. We need a sweeping, God-breathed, Spirit-anointed, devil-defeating revival!

How can we find it? Like Elijah of old, we could look for Jehovah in the *wind*. At Pentecost, after all, a rushing wind filled the place. We could look for Him in the *fire*. Did not tongues of fire come to rest upon each person? We could look for Him in the *earthquake*. Following prayer, the place where Jesus' followers met literally shook. "Yes, Lord, that's what we want! We want the rushing wind, the tongues of fire, the shaking, and the quaking!"

As wonderful as Pentecost was, however, it did not come until after many days of quiet waiting for the promise. For Elijah, it was not until he tuned in to the still, small voice, or gentle whisper (NIV), that God actually revived his flagging spirit. And that is how God usually reaches us, too. He speaks softly and tenderly in a quiet voice—not generally one we hear with our physical ears. He communicates instead in a conversation of the heart.

As Christian women, our walk with God begins in the deep reaches of our hearts. From that beginning, the journey that follows is also of the heart. We may experience some spectacular manifestations of His grace along the way, but the substance of our faith does not reside in them. God whispers to our hearts; He enlightens the eyes of our hearts (Ephesians 1:18); He communicates His love within our hearts (Romans 5:5); we offer our responses from our hearts (Psalm 27:8; 28:7). Yes, our relationship with God is, from beginning to end, heart to heart.

Most of us know we need a mighty move of God. Some of us cry out desperately for it, go to meetings, read books, listen to tapes. We pray and even fast. But revival comes not so much from activities or emotions or from being in the right place at the right time. In a sustained spiritual outpouring, *the heart of the matter is much more a matter of the heart.*

Isaiah prophesied, "A voice of one calling: 'In the desert prepare the way for the LORD'" (Isaiah 40:3). Malachi proclaimed, "See, I will send my messenger, who will prepare the way before me" (Malachi 3:1). God sent John the Baptist to fulfill these prophecies (Matthew 3:3). What was "the way" that John prepared? His essential ministry was to prepare hearts to receive Christ's ministry.

The angel Gabriel, quoting Malachi, said that John's ministry would " . . . turn the hearts of . . . the disobedient to the wisdom of the righteous—to make ready a people prepared for the Lord" (Luke 1:17). Before the great manifestation of Christ could take place, people's hearts had to be prepared. The Bible mentions hearts some 750 times, and, as a matter of fact, the entire Bible has to do with human hearts and God's compassionate efforts to reach them, to work in them, and to fill them.

As significant a role as gifts and abilities play, they are only of secondary importance. This series, therefore, is not about gifts but about hearts. If we want to see God's church in America truly restored to a brightly shining beacon in our culture, the *hearts* of His people must change, for revival is essentially a work of His grace in hearts. What kind of person does God touch, heal, and empower? What kind of person experiences enduring revival? We intend to make the answers to these questions simple and clear by surveying the hearts of various biblical women. We will see their responses to God and God's response to them. As you get to know these women better, you will be able to apply the lessons to your own life.

Spiritual rejuvenation has a cost. Most of us would prefer to walk an easy, painless path of blissful communion. If only God would just strew our way with delightful miracles and manifestations of His favor! But instead He chooses to perfect us by chiseling away at our self-nature, thus building character and making us strong, victorious, and fit for our future home in heaven. Our hearts have everything to do with His success in this endeavor.

The heart of our nation must return to God, the heart of the church must return to God, and our hearts as individuals must return to God. So let us "prepare the way" of the Lord by opening our hearts to the restoring, renewing work of His Spirit. With hearts that are healthy and rightly aligned, we can expect God's grace to raise up an army of women prepared to usher in the mighty spiritual awakening so urgently needed.

# ACKNOWLEDGMENTS

Thanks to my husband, Dr. Clayton Ford, for his insights and help with editing. Without his patient and loving support I would not have written this book. Also, thanks to my sister, Gayle Anderson, for offering her expertise with several chapters.

I would be lost without those who prayed for me. Thanks to my E-mail buddies who partnered with me in prayer: Pat Schmitz, Janine Kramer, Jean Bailes, Terry Temple, Sharon Schlotzhauer, Jean Wilson, Kathleen DeVita, Lory Chaves, Helen Mooradkanian, Kersti Stoen, Linda Storm, Cheri Cole, and my wonderful mother-in-law, Virginia Ford, and my daughter Hannah. Also, the brothers and sisters at Arcata First Baptist Church are an awesome church family. Thank you for praying me through this project. Your partnership was of inestimable worth. I love you all!

How grateful I am to the Lord for opening the door of opportunity to me to work with Crossway Books. I praise the Lord for Marvin Padgett and the other Crossway staff for whom I have gained a profound respect. I greatly appreciate their dedication to excellence. Thanks especially to my friends Lila Bishop, a genius of an editor, and to Jill Carter who, having too much to do, always makes time for me.

Above all, praise and glory go to the Lord Jesus Christ, who deserves full credit for giving us eternal life and hope. Thank You, Lord, for living in my heart.

# INTRODUCTION

When I was sixteen years old, I fantasized about becoming a famous singer, and I set out to write my first song. Not certain where to begin, I thought about the thing in life that I most wanted, the thing I thought would fulfill and complete me. Not yet a Christian, I was certain that the one thing I needed more than anything else was a boyfriend—someone to love me and to whom I could give my love. I decided to work on a happy song of love found, not a sad one of love lost. So wistfully I began to write, "Treasure, treasure, my heart's treasure, O that is you. . . . "

Reflected in these words was an innate knowledge that my yearning heart must hold treasure. Years came and went, however, and the beautiful "treasure" I longed for never materialized. Searching in all the wrong places, my heart became damaged and corrupted. It filled up with anger, rebellion, despair, and a host of other wrong attitudes. But God, by His grace, reached down and touched my heart. He showed me that He Himself was the Treasure I had always hungered for. He came into my heart, cleansed it, and began to replace all the ugliness with His eternal riches.

God created our hearts to hold the marvelous treasures of His eternal love and life. When we "open our hearts" to Christ, receiving Him as Savior and Lord, we receive the *"glorious riches"* that Paul speaks of when he refers to *"Christ in you, the hope of glory"* (Colossians 1:27). In Christ *"are hidden all the treasures of wisdom and knowledge"* (Colossians 2:3). When Christ comes into our lives, He brings His treasures with Him. It pleases Him to share His rich treasures with us; indeed He wants them revealed to us, in us, and through us. Consequently, our hearts are designed to become spiritual "treasure troves."

While some people truly experience this blessed condition of heart, others have hearts that prevent them from enjoying any spiritual progress. These spiritually impaired hearts have some form of disablement or spiritual defect that prevents them from reaching out and obtaining or retaining the glorious riches that God has given us in Christ. Instead they embrace the wrong kind of treasure.

This is a book about hearts and the treasures they contain. An old proverb says, "Faces we see; hearts we know not." The biblical record, however, allows us to see past the faces of numerous women and into their hearts. We have chosen to examine in depth a number of biblical women with healthy hearts, identifying a wholesome aspect of their character. We will compare each of these women with another woman who suffered from some heart impairment. We will see lives of virtue and victory contrasted with lives of self-destruction and defeat; women whose hearts gave place to God and His bounteous spiritual wealth are contrasted with women whose uncorrected hearts left them spiritually impoverished and holding corrupt treasure. In these hearts we see the difference between blessing and curse, triumph and tragedy.

As you get to know these women and their hearts better, you will look at your own heart, seeing strengths to embrace and weaknesses to renounce. Please open your heart to the Holy Spirit's presence and work. Let Him shine His spotlight in your hidden places. If He reveals some heart impairment in you, I hope you will respond to His conviction in a way that brings healing and restoration. God loves you and wants to heal you. He wants to help you separate and sift out worthless treasure so you can receive and carry His true, priceless, and enduring spiritual treasure.

Jesus said, "No good tree bears bad fruit, nor again does a bad tree bear good fruit; for each tree is known by its own fruit. Figs are not gathered from thorns, nor are grapes picked from a bramble bush. The good person out of the good treasure of the heart produces good, and the evil person out of evil treasure produces evil; for it is out of the abundance of the heart that the mouth speaks. Why do you call me, 'Lord, Lord,' and do not do what I tell you?" (Luke 6:43-46 NRSV).

God wants to bless us and to use our lives for His glory. Yet His success depends on our hearts—whether, as vessels for noble purposes, we pour out blessings and produce good fruit; or whether we waste our lives, producing worthless fruit, or worse, produce evil. As we respond to the Lord, forsaking our impairments and embracing godly character, we will increasingly become vessels filled to overflowing with His glorious kingdom riches. We will have experienced true revival; He will have truly become Lord of our hearts. And He will be our heart's treasure.

---

*The kingdom of heaven is like treasure hidden in a field. When a man found it, he hid it again, and then in his joy went and sold all he had and bought that field.*

MATTHEW 13:44

---

# 1

## Mary Magdalene

### THE YIELDED HEART

MATTHEW 27:55-56, 61; 28:1-10; MARK 15:40, 47; 16:1-11;
LUKE 8:1-3; 24:1-11; JOHN 19:25; 20:1-2, 10-18

MARY MAGDALENE'S STORY IS forever intertwined with the pivotal event of all time—the resurrection of our Lord Jesus Christ. She was the first to see Him risen from the dead, and she was the first person He commissioned to herald the glorious news. Why was this seemingly ordinary woman so incredibly privileged? What was it about her that caused God to show her such amazing favor? Surely the answer must lie somewhere in her heart.

---

*"Yield your hearts to the Lord, the God of Israel"*

JOSHUA 24:23

---

Hers was The Yielded Heart, fully given to Christ's lordship. For Mary, Jesus Christ was everything. He had become her Master, her life's passion, her heart's treasure. To love and serve Him with all her heart—this was her all-consuming mission in life.

Although the facts of Mary's life remain sketchy, one thing is clear: Mary loved her Lord, and the Lord loved Mary. What we know about her suggests that before meeting Christ, she must have had an unhappy and disturbed existence. The Bible says seven demons had possessed her (Luke 8:2). That would be enough to make anyone miserable! We have no way of knowing the severity of the effect on her personality. Did she suffer intolerable multiple personalities and uncontrollable outbursts? Or had she learned to cover the demons' existence enough to live a somewhat normal life externally, perhaps even working and becoming a woman of some means? We do not know.

Whatever the case, the sketchy information about Mary's past has led many to consider her the tearfully repentant woman of Luke 7. Such speculation, from medieval times, gave the English language an alteration of Mary's name—*maudlin*—meaning "effusively or tearfully sentimental." Most scholars today, however, believe it unfair to classify Mary as a harlot simply because she needed deliverance from demons.

Mary's hometown of Magdala was a fishing village on the north-western shore of the Sea of Galilee. Today Magdala is the modern city of Mejdel. Magdala was a small town, and in small towns people with serious problems rarely go unnoticed. Rigid expectations of order and propriety could make one plagued by demons doubly miserable. If this were Mary's case, people would at best avoid her and perhaps ridicule and even reject her. With her life violated by dark spiritual powers beyond her ability to understand or remove, she probably felt hopelessly defeated.

But there *was* hope for Mary! Hundreds of years before, God made a promise through the prophet Isaiah to the region of Galilee: "Nevertheless, there will be *no more gloom* for those who were in distress. In the past he humbled the land of Zebulun and the land of Naphtali, but in the future He will honor Galilee of the Gentiles, by the way of the sea, along the Jordan—The people walking in darkness have seen *a great light*; on those living in the land of the shadow of death *a light has dawned*" (Isaiah 9:1-2, emphasis added).

What a promise! And more wonderful—the time of fulfillment had come! The Light of the World was dawning in Galilee. A thirty-year-old Galilean from Nazareth was about to begin His public ministry. The Spirit of God stirred Jesus of Nazareth to leave Galilee in search of John the Baptist by whom He must be baptized. Following His baptism, Jesus returned to Galilee. Immediately upon entering the region, He began proclaiming, "The time has come! The kingdom of God is near! Repent and believe the good news!" (Mark 1:14-15).

Rather than returning to live in Nazareth where He grew up,

Jesus took up residence in Capernaum of Galilee. Teaching in a synagogue one day, He utterly amazed His listeners. As if to punctuate His incredible claims, right there in the synagogue before everyone, He cast a demon out of a man. No one fell asleep in church that day! Jesus immediately "made the headlines." News about Him spread like wildfire throughout the villages of Galilee. People everywhere talked about the new rabbi.

Large crowds began to follow Jesus everywhere He went. As He traveled from place to place, He taught, preached, and dramatically healed many. He called people to become disciples. Doubtless, Mary heard the exciting stories early in His ministry. After all, Magdala was located only three miles south of Capernaum. Mary must have wondered if this Jesus could hold the answer to her own tortured heart's need.

Perhaps numbers of times Mary had considered venturing out to see Jesus for herself, but her demons had successfully resisted her efforts. One day, however, a breakthrough came when the hunger in her heart overrode the will of the demons. It was her day of destiny, and all the devils in hell could not prevent it. We do not really know how or when Mary and Jesus met; we just know they did. Perhaps it happened something like this:

Streams of people eagerly made their way to see Jesus, and Mary joined them. Word was that the Teacher planned to address them this day from the hillside just outside Capernaum. All the excitement helped Mary temporarily forget her inner turmoil. Like a magnet, a power far greater than every opposing force drew her.

When she arrived, she sat somewhere on the crowd's fringe. *Then she saw Him!* Jesus, the prophet from Galilee, a man some said might be the long-awaited Anointed One, stood to speak. A reverent hush fell over them all. Spellbound, everyone eagerly listened as Jesus authoritatively began proclaiming God's truth and pronouncing His blessings to them.

"Blessed are the poor in spirit, for theirs is the Kingdom of heaven." Mary thought, *Could He mean me?* She recognized her own poverty of spirit. Such poverty of spirit easily makes room for kingdom treasure. The demons could see this and immediately did what demons do. They got agitated. Fighting, chiding, clawing at her insides, they argued, "The kingdom of heaven will never be for one such as you!"

"Blessed are those who mourn, for they will be comforted." A deep awareness of her spiritual need gripped Mary's heart. In the light of Jesus, she found herself grieving over her lost and despicable condition. Just seeing Him made her tremble. She was a sinner and a failure. "Will this righteous man even notice one like me? Is there hope—even for me?"

"No! Never! You are just too bad!" The agitated demons' condemnation kept stabbing at her already thrashed soul. Still, she kept listening to Jesus.

"Blessed are the meek, for they will inherit the earth." Despite her inner turmoil, in the meekness of her heart, Mary quietly submitted to the Master's teaching. Realizing their danger, the demons cried, "Listen to us! For this man will humiliate you in front of everyone!" She somehow resisted her impulses to flee.

"Blessed are those who hunger and thirst for righteousness, for they will be filled." Mary's hunger and thirst became so intense that, while her demons screamed, "Run for your life," she could no longer watch from afar. She slowly but intentionally made her way forward. While not entirely understanding His words, she did perceive that Jesus held the key to her life.

It was getting late; the crowds dispersed. Mary, however, stayed. She pushed against the human tide. She had to meet Jesus; she had to know Him. Then it happened! His eyes met hers. And what did they see as they gazed into each other's eyes? Jesus, peering deep inside, saw a broken and lonely heart pleading for help, an open and responsive heart prepared to surrender all to His lordship. Mary, for her part, perceived that Jesus was seeing right through to the core of her being. She felt ashamed. Still, rather than driving her away, something about those piercing and holy eyes captivated her—a certain tenderness, a loving concern, and a compassion that she had never before experienced.

This did not mean that the dark spirits in Mary went undetected. Jesus saw each of them—menacing, twisting, tormenting the poor woman's soul. And the demons knew He saw them. Being as intelligent as they are foul, they knew they were no match for God's Son. They tried to hide, but how could they? The Light penetrated their darkness, and they were terrified. Mary felt their terror.

Unable to contain her distress, Mary's face contorted. Battling enormous impulses to flee, by sheer willpower (and God's grace, no doubt), she resolved to keep her appointment. The demons hissed and glared at Jesus through Mary's eyes. But this was no problem for the divine Son of God who, with the Father, had already driven them from heaven.

Realizing their fate, the demons began writhing and convulsing. Suddenly and with undeniable authority, Jesus wielded His divine scalpel. "Release her!" He commanded with a power that shook hell itself. The demons had no choice. All seven went screaming away, leaving no wake behind them—only peace. The surgery complete, the Great Physician gently took His patient's hand. "They are gone now. You are free to follow Me."

Oh, what joy, what relief, filled Mary's heart. She was clean, free, buoyant. From that moment, she was a new woman. Jesus took her shame; He lifted her head. She stood forgiven, delivered from Satan's power to God's power, her old ways past. The fractures of her heart were saturated with and mended by His love. Jesus had met all her need, and she recognized her eternal debt of gratitude to Him. How could she ever do enough for Jesus?

Mary gladly enthroned Christ, the lover of her soul. He captured her heart forever, and nothing could seduce her away from Him. He had become her heart's treasure. Jesus told a parable about treasure found in a field for which a person would joyfully sell all (Matthew 13:44). Mary sold everything for Jesus—her way of life, her comforts, her home. She would follow Him to the ends of the earth. She would never turn from following her Master—never.

Mary quickly joined Jesus' inner circle of friends. The Bible says that as Jesus traveled from one town to another, proclaiming the glad tidings of God's kingdom, the twelve were with Him, along with some women. Mary heads the list of these women, all helping to support Christ's ministry out of their own resources (Luke 8:1-3). While men were generally the ones with the means to give aid, women in Jewish culture sometimes served as supporters of religious teachers. Mary and other women had benefited from Christ's ministry and, therefore, zealously endeavored to give back to Him.

Yet traveling with Jesus and the disciples and providing for the men's needs meant much more to the women than simply lending support. They, too, were disciples. Jesus permitted Mary and her friends to travel with Him and to learn alongside the men. This likely troubled the religious and cultural leaders; it probably baffled even His own disciples. Here we see how amazingly revolutionary Jesus Christ was in His treatment of women.

In Jewish culture women were second-class citizens. The welcoming of women from a position of subservience into eternally significant fellowship and service just would not seem right to many. Today, particularly in areas where the other major world religions dominate, women generally remain oppressed in the name of their gods and prophets. Jesus Christ dramatically elevated the women's standing, and in so doing He lifted us all. How radically different is the Christ of Christianity!

After the account of Mary's early experiences with Jesus, her story falls silent for several years. But surely she was never far from Him. She and the other women happily labored behind the scenes in their Master's mission. As an early disciple, Mary must have seen His miracles and heard His teachings. She surely came to know Him well, feeling the thrill of His victories and the pain of His rejections. She planned to spend the rest of her life traveling with Him. She would have it no other way.

Yet Mary could not have it her way. Dramatic changes were coming that would turn her joy to sadness. A cold wind kicked up, and out on the horizon the sky darkened. Her Master seemed more serious, more intense. With the religious leaders' rejection of Him becoming more evident, their denunciations more vocal, He even began to speak of His impending death. Worse, against all apparent reason, He resolved to leave Galilee for Jerusalem, the place of greatest danger. While Mary and her friends felt apprehension, they continued to follow Him, resolving to help in whatever ways they could (Matthew 27:55b).

As the party entered Jerusalem, Jesus met an incredible reception—palm leaves, "hosannas," everything a conquering hero might receive! No doubt the emotions of Jesus' followers soared from fearful uncertainty to heavenly optimism as their Master rode the donkey into town. Talk of death was all but forgotten. Their elation would be short-lived, however. The inconceivable was about to take place.

Late Thursday evening, just four days after their extraordinary entry into Jerusalem, disaster struck. Having concluded their Passover meal, Jesus and His friends went to Gethsemane to pray. Suddenly a mob came and arrested Jesus. His friends scarcely had time to cope with this reality when by morning's light He had already appeared before the Sanhedrin and was condemned to die.

The chief priests and city elders were unanimous. They spat on Jesus while mocking and beating Him. Then they led Him off to Pilate for more abuse and humiliation. Pilate could have released Him, but the crowd that had a few days earlier been singing "Hosanna" were this day shouting, "Crucify Him!" Pilate washed his hands and turned Jesus over to mocking soldiers, who shoved a thorny crown onto His head. They cruelly drove Him through Jerusalem's streets to Golgotha where they stripped Him of His clothing and dignity. Then they crucified Him, driving spikes into His wrists and feet and hanging Him high upon a rough-hewn Roman cross—all this by Friday noon.

These events must have devastated Mary. Fools crazed by deception and jealousy had obviously fabricated the horrid accusations against Jesus. But what could Mary do? She could not address the Sanhedrin or appeal to Pilate. She could not convince the mob that had turned against Him or fight off the guards who abused Him. She could not even minister to Jesus' personal needs, try as she might. No, this was a road Jesus must travel alone.

Unable to do what she would, Mary did what she could. At His popularity's height, she had surrendered her heart to Him. Now at

His popularity's collapse, she refused to reclaim that yielded heart. Along with Mary, the wife of Clopas, and the disciple John, she joined Jesus' mother and aunt at the cross (John 19:25).

While family and friends generally attended executions, this one involved much controversy and danger. John may have felt some safety from prosecution because of his youth. Mary, too, was much less likely to be indicted than were the male disciples. Still, she must have felt danger. Even so, she boldly remained there while all disciples but John were nowhere to be seen. She may have thought, "Have I come so far, followed so long, experienced so much, and loved so passionately that I should now desert my Lord?"

Mary knew Jesus needed the support of friends at that moment more than ever, and she committed herself to be there for Him. Yet what overwhelming pain and grief must have seized her heart as she witnessed His agony. The heart so graciously healed was again torn apart. Still, even if it were ripped to shreds, each shred would enthrone Christ. It must have comforted Jesus to know that Mary's heart fully belonged to Him from beginning to end—and the brutal end had indeed come. Jesus quietly exhaled a final breath and died.

Immediately after Jesus' death, miraculous things happened—darkness, an earthquake, and even dead people rising (Matthew 27:51-53). Imagine the commotion! Yet Mary kept her focus. She, along with the other Mary, followed Joseph of Arimathea to see just where he would take Jesus' body. What a small and unseemly funeral procession these few made. Hardly a funeral for a King. No music, no official prayers, no lovely words spoken over the deceased. Joseph placed Jesus inside the tomb and had the great stone rolled against it. After this, he left. All was then quiet except perhaps for the sobs of the women as they lingered.

Mary intended to honor the Lord by anointing His body with spices and perfumes. He died, however, just before the Sabbath, so she had to postpone the anointing. The Sabbath was a strictly enforced day of rest, and that meant no visits to the tomb. She must purchase and prepare the spices Saturday night after the Sabbath ended. The preparations took time, so this meant Mary must wait until Sunday morning to visit the tomb.

The Synoptic Gospels tell us that other women accompanied Mary to the tomb Sunday morning, but John's Gospel fails to mention the others. John mentions Mary alone because she is the primary participant, the most active, the most passionate. Again and again she proves her heart's unswerving devotion to her Master—a devotion far stronger than death.

Caring for Jesus was Mary's only concern while in Jerusalem. She probably slept little that Saturday night. According to John's account (John 20), she rose early Sunday morning while it was still dark and went straight to the grave site. But upon arriving, she was shocked to find the heavy stone moved away from the tomb. This must have terrified her; turning, she ran. Finding Peter and John, she cried, "They have taken the Lord out of the tomb, and we don't know where they have put Him!" The two disciples raced there, and once inside, they too found the tomb empty. Unsure of what to do, they simply went home. Mary had not understood Jesus' statement that He must die and then rise again on the third day. Now in her despair, she could not remember it. She needed help, but where could she turn? She just stood there, weeping her heart out.

She bent one more time to look inside the tomb. What a surprise greeted her! Inside, two gleaming angels dressed in white were seated where Jesus' body had rested. "Woman," they asked, "why are you crying?"

"They have taken my Lord away, and I don't know where they have put Him." Remarkably, Mary remained far more concerned with finding Jesus than with seeing angels. Turning from them, she saw someone standing behind her whom she took to be the gardener.

"Woman, why are you crying?" He then asked, "Who is it you are looking for?"

"Sir," she replied, "if you have carried Him away, tell me where you have put Him, and I will get Him."

"Mary," He spoke tenderly. Blinded by grief, she hadn't at first recognized Him. But hearing her name stopped her heart. In that instant of confusion and jubilant recognition, she must have nearly fainted. What? How . . . ? It was . . . Jesus! He was ALIVE! That wonderful moment made her the first eyewitness to Christ's resurrection. Leaving it to the angels to share the glad tidings with Mary had not satisfied Him. His affection for Mary was such that He personally wanted to comfort and satisfy her with His presence.

We can only imagine the inexpressible joy that rushed over her heart. "Master!" she cried. She wanted to run to Him and affectionately embrace Him, smothering His feet with kisses and tears.

"Do not hold me, for I have not yet returned to the Father," He instructed. Then He gave her one of the most wonderful assignments in all of human history. "Go instead to my brothers and tell them, 'I am returning to my Father, and your Father, to my God and your God.'" Mary would be the first to testify to Christ's resurrection.

She could have leaped a wall! Casting aside her now useless spices, she must have nearly flown from the tomb to herald the glorious news. Mary exploded through the door where the disciples were hiding for the second time in one morning. Ecstatically she announced to the astonished listeners, *"I have seen the Lord!"*

Mark's Gospel concurs with John's regarding who first saw the Lord alive. "When Jesus rose early the first day of the week, He appeared first to Mary Magdalene, out of whom He had driven seven demons. She went and told those who had been with Him and who were mourning and weeping." Mark goes on to say, "When they heard that Jesus was alive and that she had seen Him, they did not believe it" (Mark 16:9-11).

What! Jesus had repeatedly told His disciples He would die and rise again. They were no doubt aware of the mysterious circumstances surrounding His death—the dark skies, the earthquake, and people rising from their graves. Peter and John had themselves seen Jesus' empty tomb. Why then could not one of them have believed Mary's testimony?

It is true that they had suffered grief and confusion, but could it partly be that the messenger was a woman? Why, after all, would the Lord appear first to a woman—any woman? Why would He send *her* to tell *them*, the apostles? If an apostle is a messenger of the good news, Mary was acting like an apostle to the apostles—a hard pill to swallow. A woman's testimony meant little in Judaism, and the apostles surely thought this report was the delusion of a well-meaning but hysterical woman.

In truth, Jesus was again turning cultural norms on their head. In appearing first to Mary, He tacitly rebuked the disciples. He also wanted to reward this dear woman for her heart's constancy. Her faithfulness to Him did not end with His death, for many waters cannot quench love; neither can floods drown it (Song of Songs 8:7). She had never forsaken Him as the men had. Peter and John had that morning gone away from the tomb; but Mary had remained, still diligently seeking Him. Just as Jesus had promised to those who seek, He let Mary find Him. Because Mary followed Jesus to the bitter end of His humiliation, she was granted to see the glorious beginning of His exaltation.

Mary Magdalene, faithful disciple of the Lord Jesus Christ, was the first eyewitness of Christ's resurrection, the central event on which the Christian faith hinges; she was the first to open her heart to the resurrected Christ; she was the first to receive the magnificent commission to tell of the Savior's triumph over death; and she was the first to proclaim the good news of the greatest event of history. What a privilege she enjoyed! And it all began when her heart melted, and she gave up the reins of her life, saying, "Yes, Lord; I yield my life to You. You are the love of my life; I'm all Yours."

## LESSONS FOR OUR OWN HEARTS

> *" . . . but in your hearts reverence Christ as Lord."*
>
> 1 PETER 3:15 RSV

Mary's life offers us an important lesson about hearts. The key to true dedication to Christ never lies in a heart's own inherent goodness. Mary's heart, like our own, had plenty of impurities. The key rather can be found in a heart's ability to open itself and be emptied of all else except the love of Christ. This takes full surrender to Him. Only then will He sweep the heart clean and refill it with His goodness and life.

Those, like Mary, who fill their hearts with love for Jesus and keep them yielded to His lordship, even in times of seeming hopeless gloom, are those whose hearts receive rich reward. It is into these Christ-enthroning hearts that He pours an abundance of His love. The Lord reserves for them the sweetest revelations of His grace. Their lives become ones of manifest miracles; they gain entrance into a new and increasingly bright day. Mary's heart and life bear this out. Fully yielding her heart to Christ, she received and was filled with the richest of His kingdom treasures.

Does your relationship with Christ often seem like a back-and-forth tug-of-war that leaves you with little spiritual progress? Perhaps what needs resolving is the issue of lordship. Jesus Christ—is He the Lord of your heart? An unyielding heart, out of harmony with Him and His purposes, cannot hope for peace with God. True and lasting satisfaction comes only through wholehearted surrender.

I know someone whose home is crammed with thrift store bargains. By and large, the stuff serves no purpose and has no real value. Can you imagine the foolishness of keeping a house so full of junk that though plenty of money is available for purchasing quality furnishings, there is no room for them? What if this were your home? Year after year it remains stuffed with meaningless old knick-knacks, bric-a-brac, keepsakes, and clutter. You long for the day when you can do something with the mess, but some twisted loyalty to these things prevents you. You simply cannot bring yourself to effect any change. You are simply too overwhelmed by the magnitude of the problem. You have even secretly wished the house would just burn down so you could start over.

One day, out of nowhere, someone presents you with an amazing offer. A world-famous decorator sees great promise in your house and wants to redecorate it at no charge to you. Promising to make it a showpiece, he says he will do a work that causes not only you to marvel but also everyone who sees it. He assures you that upon completion, you will love to live in your house. He even promises to donate some priceless furnishings to the cause. Wow! What a deal!

Oh . . . he does have one condition. He will only do his work on *his* terms—not yours. He is the one with the expertise; he is the one who knows exactly what to do. And he makes it clear that he will not just shuffle your junk around a bit. Every bit of it must go! Only then will he begin to scrub, paper, repair, repaint, re-tile, and refurnish your house with his unique and priceless treasures. Realizing your weakness, he even offers to come and clear out the house for you. Now would you jump at this opportunity, or would you fret and argue with him over what you must give up?

Doesn't Christ cleanse, restore, and refurnish hearts? Isn't He the world's greatest interior designer? Indeed He is, and He wants to go to work. Yet while many refuse Him all right to enter, others welcome Him in but keep bickering with Him over what they will allow Him to remove. They never quite make enough room for His blessings.

---

*What is more,* I consider everything a loss *compared to the surpassing greatness of knowing Christ Jesus my Lord, for whose sake I have lost all things.* I consider them rubbish.

PHILIPPIANS 3:8, *emphasis added*

---

How about you? Are you willing to let Him throw out your junk? If you would fully receive from the Lord, you must yield completely. This is the essence of trusting the Lord with all your heart. The old trappings must be removed, the old nature stripped away.

Do you trust Jesus Christ? Do you realize just how much He loves you? Mary took the leap of faith into His care and keeping. She quickly discovered His profound love. In the beauty and purity of that love, she found wholeness. Christ's love for Mary was limitless. If she were the only person in all the world who needed salvation, He gladly would have died for her.

Likewise, His love for you defies comprehension. He would have died for you alone, too. He loves you that much. Mary gladly surrendered her heart to follow such a one. Can you, too, yield your willful heart to Jesus Christ?

You are so privileged! Christ wants to do a great work in you. He will do it skillfully; He will do it freely! Please allow Him to do it! Give Him your heart without reservation. Let Him throw out your worthless junk. Then you will have a greatly enlarged capacity within your heart to receive from Him. Let the love of God in Christ have full sway. Embrace His plan and purpose for your life. He has an abundance of new treasure to pour into your heart. He has miracles for you. Do as Mary did. Make room. Give Christ freedom to reign in your heart.

Let us again consider Mary. Just think of what she would have missed if, following the crucifixion, she had thought Jesus forever gone and simply given up enthroning Him. Wouldn't she have slept in Sunday morning and missed it all? Oh, but she did not! Her heart remained centered on Christ. She went early to the tomb, and because she did, she became the joyful participant in the world's first and most memorable Easter sunrise service.

## Heart Check

1. As you examine your heart, do you see hindrances that keep you from wholeheartedly trusting Christ? What action do you think God wants you to take?

2. Have you ever felt that the Lord abandoned you during a time of difficulty? Were you tempted to forsake Him? How can you keep your heart yielded to Him at such times?

3. Do you, like Mary, go to the Lord first thing in your day? Are there other less important things that habitually come first?

4. What is the most important principle you can apply to your life from Mary's example?

5. Compose a prayer to God in response to this chapter's lessons.

# 2

## THE CONTROLLING HEART

1 KINGS 16:30-31; 18:4, 13, 16-46; 19:1-5; 21:1-29;
2 KINGS 9:6-10, 22, 30-37; REVELATION 2:20-24.

HOW MANY OF US HAVE DAUGHTERS named Jezebel? Probably not a one. Have you ever known anyone named Jezebel? There is a reason for that, of course. What loving mother, after all, would choose to name her baby daughter after someone who ranks as the most wicked woman in the Bible, a woman whose very name is synonymous with evil?

---

"The memory of the righteous is a blessing, *but the name of the wicked will rot*"

PROVERBS 10:7, emphasis added

---

This infamous woman lived in the late 800s B.C. Although she came to Israel as an outsider, the daughter of a Sidonian king, her marriage to Israel's King Ahab made her queen. When she arrived as a young bride, she had every opportunity to use her influence for good. She could have studied the law, the prophets, and the miracles of her new country. She could have allowed her heart to melt in awe and reverence of the one holy and true God, bowing her heart to Him, thankful for the privilege of living in the land of promise. But Jezebel was no impressionable, sweet, young thing. From the time she set her feet on Israel's soil, she was a woman with her own agenda.

Our wise and all-knowing God had rightly warned the Israelites that if they began marrying their sons to Canaan's pagan daughters, the foreign gods of these women would surely lead Israel astray (Exodus 34:12-16). And what was Canaan's most popular god? Baal.

Jezebel, like her father Ethbaal,[1] was a Baal worshiper. Baal's name means "master," "possessor," or "husband." Besides being a nature god of rain and thunder, Baal was a god of strength and fertility, symbolized by a bull. The sensuous nature of Baal worship, with its tantalizing ritual prostitution, easily seduced fickle-hearted Israel. Turning from the God of his fathers, King Ahab joined his wife in Baal worship. Before long, her influence corrupted the entire nation. Under Jezebel's demonic obsession, worship of Baal (and the mother-goddess Asherah) experienced a revival such as had not been seen since God had led His people to enter the Promised Land.

What kind of heart did Jezebel possess? We see in her the antithesis of Mary's yielded heart. While both women were passionately devoted, one committed herself to Christ's sovereignty and the other to self. Because Jezebel's heart stayed riveted to its throne, serving itself alone, we call her heart The Controlling Heart. Completely controlling her own kingdom, Jezebel clasped tightly to the reins of power, ruling with an iron fist. Her unyielding heart provided no place for God or His rich kingdom treasures. Rejecting His truth, she poisoned her subjects against the Holy One and their precious heritage.

Jezebel must have learned much from her father, who murdered his brother to become king of Tyre and Sidon. Like him, his daughter had no scruples about dealing ruthlessly with anyone who got in her way. Converting Israel to paganism satisfied her little. She would not be content until she had destroyed every semblance of the Hebrew faith and had murdered every one of God's prophets. She nearly succeeded! Meanwhile, no fewer than 450 priests of Baal feasted daily at her table.

Jezebel proved to be the despotic power behind Ahab's throne. The king yielded to his domineering wife, becoming essentially her puppet. God's Word says of these two, "There was never a man like

Ahab, who sold himself to do evil in the eyes of the Lord, urged on by Jezebel his wife" (1 Kings 21:25).

Yet Jezebel had made a fatal blunder in underestimating God and the lowly servant He had placed in her destructive path. Despite her bloody campaign, she could not destroy the prophet Elijah, who enjoyed God's providential care. Standing resolutely for the Lord, he became Jezebel's chief adversary. A single man or woman of God can cause havoc in the kingdom of darkness, and Elijah was up for the challenge.

One day he boldly approached King Ahab and demanded a contest between Jezebel's 450 prophets of Baal and himself—that is 450 to one![2] The king must have thought this would make for great entertainment. He summoned not only the entire company of prophets but also all of Israel to witness the event. Who would prevail: Yahweh, the God of Elijah, or Baal, the god of Jezebel?

All Israel showed up for the cosmic showdown—except, surprisingly, Jezebel herself. With everyone assembled, Elijah called out, "How long will you waver between two opinions? If the LORD is God, then follow him; but if Baal is God, follow him!" (1 Kings 18:21). Elijah went on to complain that he alone remained as the Lord's prophet. The people must have wondered what this scrawny little man could do against the huge company of Baal's prophets.

Elijah issued this challenge: There would be two bulls, one for Jezebel's prophets to sacrifice to their god and one for Elijah to sacrifice to his. Neither side, however, could light the fire for the burnt offering. Then he challenged, "You call on the name of your god, and I will call on the name of the LORD. The God who answers by fire—he is God."

Jezebel's prophets went first, calling on Baal from morning till noon. "O, Baal, answer us!" they cried. But Baal's lips remained sealed, the heavens as still as death. Elijah began to taunt them. "Shout louder," he urged. "Perhaps he is deep in thought, or busy, or traveling. Maybe he is sleeping and must be awakened." So they shouted all the louder, raving on and on, cutting themselves in tribute to their god until the site was a bloody mess. Despite their frantic devotion, Baal failed to respond.

Then it was Elijah's turn. Adding insults to their already serious injuries, he made them wait while he repaired the Lord's ruined altar, dug a trench around it, added wood, and prepared his offering. Then he doused the altar, the offering, and all the wood three times with water until it filled the trench. That done, he simply prayed to the Lord, "O LORD, God of Abraham, Isaac and Israel, let it be known today that you are God in Israel and that I am your servant and have done all these things at your command. Answer me, O, LORD, answer me, so these people will know that you, O LORD, are God, and that you are turning their hearts back again" (1 Kings 18:36-37).

Immediately the fire of God fell, consuming the offering, the wood, the water in the trench, and even the stones. Thus ended one of the most dramatic contests in history. The scales came off Israel's eyes. The nation came to its senses. Elijah put Baal's false prophets to death on the spot. The people fell prostrate and shouted, "The LORD—he is God! The LORD—he is God!"

Even Ahab must have been caught up in the excitement. Still Elijah wanted him to see a further demonstration of God's sovereign power. Several years prior, Elijah had stood before Ahab to pronounce drought upon the land. The drought came, and it was severe. But this day of new beginnings was one for celebrating. Elijah told Ahab, "Go eat and drink, for there is the sound of heavy rain."

So Ahab left Mount Carmel—probably ready to party. As he neared his palace, though, he must have remembered his wife and, feeling queasy, suffered a sudden loss of appetite. Elijah's God might send a rainstorm outside, but what would he do with the storm await-ing him inside his door? How would he explain the day's events to Jezebel?

Not only did the king likely go to bed without dinner that night, but the revival of Yahweh worship also meant serious trouble for Elijah. Baal's prophets had been no ordinary men. They had been Jezebel's personal prophets. They had always told the queen what she wanted to hear. They had deified the king and queen, adulating them and exclusively prophesying power and glory for them. What a terri-ble loss for Jezebel! Not only were her prophets dead, but they had shamed the queen by losing the contest and exposing themselves as frauds. Wouldn't she finally repent of her Baal worship after suffering such a humiliating defeat?

Hardly! Don't try bothering a woman like Jezebel with facts. In her mind the contest had not ended on the mountain. Her idols could fail, but *she* would not! Baal could succumb, but she would prevail. Elijah's God proved himself by fire and rain. So what? When it came down to it, Jezebel was the real god of her life, and she was not about to move over for Another.

A controlling heart is a deluded heart. Jezebel actually believed she would win her war with the Ultimate Controller. She furiously sent a messenger to Elijah with these words: "May the gods deal with me, be it ever so severely, if by this time tomorrow I do not make your life like that of one of them!"

Think of this one woman's power! Elijah had just triumphed in one of history's greatest contests. He had put 450 false prophets to death in an afternoon. Yet what happened next? Why, one threatening word from this iron-fisted, steel-hearted, fire-breathing woman, and his victory vanished away like a wisp of smoke—kapoof! God's mighty prophet, who had called down fire and then rain from heaven, suddenly became a spineless wet noodle and fled for his life! Jezebel's wrath so terrified him that he would rather have died in the wilderness than face her.

In whining self-pity, he pleaded with God to let him die. "I've had enough, Lord," he bawled. "Take my life; for I am no better than my ancestors." But Elijah was not destined to die as a faithless wimp. While wicked Jezebel seized control of nearly everything else in the kingdom, her mastery over God's prophet was short-lived. When Elijah later departed this earth, he left in a chauffeured heavenly chariot, not as Jezebel's victim.

Jezebel again displayed her controlling heart in her dealings with the man Naboth.[3] Her husband came sulking home one day after failing in his bid to purchase his neighbor's ancestral land. The king had wanted the man's vineyard for a vegetable garden, but Naboth responded, "God forbid that I should give you the inheritance of my fathers."

Ahab knew Mosaic law. The law made Naboth responsible to his descendants, past and future. To give up his land to the king would have relegated his family to the status of royal dependents. Another of God's laws forbade coveting a neighbor's land. Yet not getting his vegetable garden made Ahab so miserably unhappy that he went moping to bed without eating.

When the queen found out the reason for her husband's despondency, she could have reminded him that with all he possessed, he didn't need the field. But how could she? Her heart would never permit her to let a control issue like this simply pass. No, she must conquer! "Don't *you* govern Israel?" she purred to her husband. "Cheer up, get out of bed and eat. *I'll* get Naboth's vineyard for you."

Wasting no time, she devised an evil scheme against her unsuspecting neighbor. She sent letters in the king's name to all the leaders of Naboth's city, commanding them to proclaim a fast. They would seat Naboth prominently with a couple of liars beside him. These men would claim to have overheard Naboth cursing both God and the king. Because of the presence of two witnesses, the leaders would immediately take Naboth out and stone him to death.

The plot proceeded as planned, resulting in the murder of a man innocently and commendably obeying God's law. With the deed done, Jezebel went to her husband and told him to go take possession of Naboth's land. Would Ahab question his wife? Of course not. What Ahab appreciated about his wife was that she had everything under control—her control, it is true. He seized the field.

Soon the incident seemed behind them—Ahab enjoying his new piece of property and Jezebel enjoying tight control over her world. Major trouble, however, lay ahead for Jezebel and Ahab. You see, the word of the Lord came to Elijah and armed him with a fresh "Thus saith the Lord!" He went to Ahab pronouncing severe judgment on him for his latest sin—calamity for both Ahab and his posterity. And of the queen, he said, "Dogs will devour Jezebel by the wall of Jezreel" (1 Kings 21:23).

Now anyone with a lick of sense would be shaking in his sandal straps at hearing such a pronouncement. Ahab immediately repented.

Nothing indicates, however, Jezebel being so moved. She must have thought, *The Lord? Ha! I'll control our destiny, thank you!*

As she lived on some years after Ahab's death, we continue to see her pernicious influence on the kingdom. Her eldest son, Ahaziah, also worshiped Baal. His kingship lasted less than two years before he died. Jezebel's second son, Jehoram, succeeded him. While not a Baal worshiper, King Jehoram was still considered wicked. He ruled twelve years before the army leader, Jehu, commissioned by Elijah to overthrow the Ahab dynasty, caught up with him. When Jehoram asked Jehu if he had come in peace, the commander declared, "How can there be peace as long as all the idolatry and witchcraft of your mother Jezebel abound?"[4]

After Jehu killed Jehoram, he went to find wicked Jezebel in Jezreel, perhaps the site of the winter palace. Upon receiving word of Jehu's arrival with his forces, Jezebel must have known she would be next. She decided that if she must die, it would be with her head defiantly held high. So she put on her makeup, fixed her hair, and went to the window.

Alluding to Zimri who wiped out the house of Baasha but reigned only seven days, she hurled down an insult to Jehu. "Have you come in peace, you Zimri, murderer of your master?" But Jehu shouted, "Who is on my side? Throw her down!" Some servants threw her from the window, and there she died. Dogs ate her body before anyone could bury her, thus fulfilling Elijah's word.

---

*So you will be destroyed for not obeying the LORD your God.*

DEUTERONOMY 8:20

---

Yes, a controlling heart is a deluded heart. Although Jezebel managed to stay in the ring for a few rounds, she ultimately lost her bout with God. She died just as He said she would. Even in her final moments, foolish Jezebel was seeing to her face and hair rather than to her wicked heart.

That Jezebel's name deeply impressed the Hebrew mind may be

traced forward all the way to the book of Revelation where Christ, the risen Lord, singles out a "prophetess" in the church of Thyatira. Much like the Jezebel of old, she was a woman of power who refused to yield to Christ's lordship. Her heart, too, had become filled with evil and corruption. She also brought a heretical, idolatrous influence with her into the midst of God's people. Evidently her controlling spirit seduced many in the church away from Christ, leading them to become *her* disciples rather than His—"Her children," He called them. Christ Himself gave this woman of Thyatira the worst possible label when He said, "Nevertheless, I have this against you: You tolerate that woman Jezebel" (Revelation 2:20).

## LESSONS FOR OUR OWN HEARTS

What about us? The Bible warns us to keep our hearts with all diligence. God looks at our hearts, and He regards with pleasure only those that long to know and please Him. We may think we have such hearts, but are we being honest with ourselves? We may need to take a closer look.

We all, to some degree, wear masks—masks that permit us to form our mutual admiration clubs where we delude each other into thinking ourselves so righteous, so . . . Christian. But God is not impressed. And neither should we be. If we gaze intently into the mirror of God's law, the wretchedness of our hearts becomes evident.

The more we grow as Christians, and the nearer we draw to God, the less confident we feel about our own character. The light of His truth exposes us for what we are. About the time we see our heart approach true purity, some vileness, some poison again surfaces to burst our bubble. Just as the Bible says, "The heart is deceitful above all things and beyond cure. Who can understand it?" (Jeremiah 17:9). This speaks of your heart; it speaks of mine.

Dare we then suggest that Jezebel can be found in the church today? Dare we admit that we can even glimpse her lurking in the shadows of our own hearts? Indeed, she is here, her spirit ever stalking us. And wherever you find controlling, dominating women, you surely find Jezebel. She loves getting a toehold in the church, and many churches fall beneath her ruthless power. How often Jezebel starts rebellions in churches and wants to have her way regardless of the destruction she causes.

Have you ever been at war with God? Having convinced yourself that you knew best, did you ultimately learn you had only fooled yourself? In the midst of your rebellion, you were certain of the rightness of your cause. Then at some point, likely with your back to the floor, it became clear that you had been wrong all along. You thought you could win, but you had become instead the big loser. Until our term of service in this life expires, we will be fighting and contending. But how it behooves us to make absolutely sure we are fighting on the right side—for God and not against Him. Jesus warned, "See to it, then, that the light within you is not darkness" (Luke 11:35).

---

*Submit yourselves, then, to God.*

JAMES 4:7

*Obey your leaders and submit to their authority.*

HEBREWS 13:17

*Wives, submit to your husbands.*

COLOSSIANS 3:18

*Submit yourselves for the Lord's sake to every authority.*

1 PETER 2:13

---

Some years ago I became involved with a weekend ministry in a southern California church. God was doing a marvelous work of His grace among the church's youth. He was using the youth pastor mightily, and the winds of revival were blowing. Beautiful testimonies of dramatically changed lives flowed from the pulpit as youths testified of the glorious things God was doing in their lives. The senior pastor fully supported this beautiful work of God's Spirit, as did much of the congregation.

But a Sunday school class comprised of some folk who basically

ran the church reacted against what God was doing. They were losing control. They didn't like the testimonies, they didn't like the
music, they didn't like the joy—they didn't like God moving in and
changing things. Things had always been done a certain way, and that
is how things were going to stay. Their controlling spirit, like
Jezebel's, turned ruthless.

I was part of a team called in to try to help unify this church. After
our ministry, we thought things were beginning to pull together.
Unfortunately, however, the division only widened. Little time
passed before we received news that the youth pastor had left, and the
youth had scattered. Sometime later the senior pastor resigned also.

One day at a Christian event, I was standing in a buffet lunch line
behind some women. I overheard one woman say she was from that
particular church. Then like a conquering champion, she proudly
nodded to her friend and announced, "We got *our* church back." Her
words stabbed me to the heart, and I went home angry and grieving.

This woman and her accomplices had undermined legitimate
spiritual authority in the church until they drove their pastors out. She
thought she had won; but the church had lost, and she had lost. God's
life had gone from that place, and all that remained was an empty tomb
of a church full of dead bones. Still she had control of that tomb, and
that was what mattered! If only this woman had recognized that it was
God's light she saw on those shining young faces. If only she had
embraced them in her heart as the gifts and treasures from God that
they really were. But, no, they had threatened her kingdom. Jezebel
was not about to move over and relinquish her stubborn control.

It should frighten us to think that Jezebel could visit so close to
home. Could we, too, entertain her in our own hearts? If you see her
lurking there, you need to fall on your face before God and plead for
mercy. But never plead for mercy for Jezebel, whom we might be
tempted to protect. No! She is the one who forever stands as an example of what a woman ought not to be. She is the wicked tyrant who,
deserving no mercy, must be cast down from her lofty tower. Jezebel
must die. God says to us all: "Who is on My side? Throw her down!"

We must cry out, "Lord, have mercy on me, a sinner! Lord, let me be humble, let me be submissive, let me lay aside my stubborn pride! I step aside, Lord. I give You space to work in my husband's life, in my children's lives, in my church's life. You take charge!"

How does one become such a monstrous person as Jezebel? Perhaps it begins in infancy. Every baby begins life as an egotistical and self-preoccupied little tyrant. The whole universe revolves around queen baby. If permitted to continue unchecked in infancy, the growing sovereign heads for real trouble. If she never learns to yield her will to her parent, her ability to yield to the Lord or to anyone else becomes seriously handicapped. Trusting herself alone, such a one always clamors for control. This "control freak" may believe in God, but her God must orbit around her, not vice versa.

While we do not like thinking of ourselves as possessing even the remotest tendency toward Jezebel, I appeal again for your honesty. When we know God's will but are not ready to trust Him in it, we might naturally respond by attempting to control the situation. Letting go and trusting God can be hard to do. When we don't see things going the way we think they should, we can start doubting God's sovereignty. Often insecurity underlies a controlling spirit. "I don't trust God to take care of me, so I had better do it myself."

A missionary, Rabi Maharaj, once stayed in our home while conducting a series of meetings at the local university. This former Hindu of the Brahman caste travels the world over giving his incredible testimony of God's grace. What most impressed me about Rabi was that he is a true faith missionary. Never soliciting funds, he still travels wherever God sends him in the world. Sitting at the table with Rabi and listening as he told story after story from his faith pilgrimage, I was both exhilarated and challenged.

Once Rabi had been on his way to the airport to fly overseas before the Lord had provided the necessary funds for the flight. I said, "Rabi, I don't think I could live like that." At the same time I was longing for the kind of freedom and excitement I saw in him.

He replied, "Oh, but you are missing out on such a *wonderful* adventure." Rabi knew the adventure of controlling nothing, of leaving everything in God's hands, and of seeing miracles unfold before him every step of his way. I must confess that my heart was left in conflict with itself. I felt envy for all he had given to God; yet I felt fear that I might have to do something similar. After my encounter with Rabi, I found myself surrendering to God in deeper ways.

God has a wonderful adventure of faith for us, but we must relinquish control and trust Him. This calls for a daily walk of continually offering up fresh surrenders to Him. When Christ comes into a human heart, His lordship is not automatic. A divestiture must take place—a stripping away of the "rights" of our old self-nature's rights.

Imagine for a moment that your heart represents a kingdom, and this kingdom is inhabited by a multitude of people going about their lives and assigned duties. By the will of these people, Her Highness Queen Jezebel has lost her throne in your heart. The kingdom now belongs to King Jesus. An unresolved issue remains, however, between the King and His subjects. While overthrown, unseated, and dispossessed, Jezebel remains alive, sitting shackled in a dungeon. Although King Jesus sits enthroned in her place and greatly pleases the people, they do not want Him to slay Jezebel. For they still feel some affection for her. She was their queen, after all, and slaying her seems brutal. They think if she sits in prison for a while, she just might reform her ways. They will try to work on her while keeping her subdued and out of trouble. Given time, she will surely learn to cooperate with their wonderful new King.

Yet this pugnacious, wicked woman considers such a suggestion insulting. She will not simply lie down and die. She may be down, but she is not out. Jezebel never concedes defeat. Never! Even if she should find herself banished from the kingdom of your heart, she will find some means of fighting her way back to the throne room where she can once again seize control.

During Jezebel's reign, she had initiated many pet programs for manipulating her subjects' loyalty. Now from her dungeon, she uses her well-honed skills, sending out messages, reminding her former subjects of all the good they once enjoyed under her rule. Some of her reprobate nobles still continue in influential positions, and through them she will move the people's hearts back to her.

As long as any double-mindedness remains on the people's part toward their King, the wicked queen will find a way to wriggle her way back to the throne. She will grieve Him greatly, fomenting unrest and rebellion. Eventually, no longer convinced He looks after their best interests, the people will look to her. The call will go forth: "Restore Queen Jezebel to the throne! She cares best for us!" Jezebel will even assure the people that if they do restore her reign, she will benevolently offer their deposed King kind treatment. Because Jesus is a "good man," He can keep living in the kingdom—provided He stays confined to His assigned corner and makes no waves.

How can this kingdom crisis be solved? There is only one way. Clearly, any loyalty to Jezebel on the people's part is disloyalty to their King. For the kingdom's sake, they must stop protecting Jezebel and stand with Him. As long as she remains alive, she will plague the kingdom. Therefore, she and her co-conspirators must be executed. Yes, they must die! Only then can the kingdom enjoy lasting tranquility, order, and progress; only then can it truly prosper.

We must, in like manner, allow Christ to deal ruthlessly with every disloyal opposition to His lordship within our hearts. Becoming a Christian means that Christ becomes King of one's life. And that means submitting ourselves to an uncomfortable cleansing from all forms of corruption. The length of time this cleansing takes generally depends upon the cooperation we give our King. While the authority already belongs to Him, He will not seize it. We must yield full control of our lives to Him; we must allow Christ unconditional authority to clean up the kingdom of our hearts.

Jesus' words, "Why do you call me Lord, Lord, and not do what I say?" could be restated, "Why do you call Me your King, but not let Me take charge?" Have you let Him take charge? Is Queen Jezebel cast down in your life? Christ wants to be your Sovereign. He wants to take charge, first cleansing and then filling you with good treasure.

Let Him cleanse you; you cannot cleanse yourself. You cannot work your way into a perfect heart no matter how hard you try. Every self-motivated, legalistic effort to bring personal reformation is a guaranteed failure. Only the blood of Jesus cleanses hearts from sin, and He will do it if you fully yield control to Him. Freed of Jezebel's influence, Christ will fill your heart with delightful treasure from His own storehouse of heavenly wealth.

## Heart Check

1. Which heart would you most like to see represent your own—a yielded heart like Mary Magdalene's or a controlling heart like Jezebel's?

2. Think of a way in which God has worked in your heart. Did you first need to surrender to His lordship?

3. What steps can you take now to make your heart less controlling and more yielded?

4. What is the most important principle you can apply to your life from Jezebel's example?

5. Compose a prayer to God in response to this chapter's lessons.

# 3

## *Rahab*

### THE DISCERNING HEART

JOSHUA 2:1-21; 6:17-25; HEBREWS 11:31;
JAMES 2:25

THE ANCIENT CITY OF JERICHO—also called "the City of Palm Trees"[1]—was situated in the pleasant fertile plains near the Jordan River just west of Moab. This lovely city with its palm and balsam trees was one of the oldest cities in the world. Surviving every previous threat, its twenty-foot-thick, twenty-five-foot-high, fortified double wall made Jericho the strongest of Canaan's cities. Guards confidently stationed atop its perimeter could see for miles. A symbol of Canaanite military strength, they commonly believed Jericho to be invincible.

Two young men, however, were convinced otherwise. Full of faith, they scuttled down from the hills where they had been hiding near Jericho. Carefully slipping across the Jordan River and walking into Israel's camp, they went straight to Captain Joshua. "The Lord has surely given the whole land into our hands," they declared. "All the people are melting in fear because of us."

What gave these two such confidence? A woman of Jericho named Rahab. She had so encouraged them in their mission that after one short night, they trusted her with their lives. While she lived a dark and sinful existence, she opened her heart to treasures of truth. As a result, she perceived something hidden from the rest of her people—that the God of Israel was the true God. Having correctly read and interpreted the signs around her, she foresaw that this God would soon hand her country over to Israel. Yet she also detected the way of escape for her and her loved ones. Thus, we call Rahab's heart The Discerning Heart.

---

*The discerning heart seeks knowledge, but the mouth of a fool feeds on folly.*

PROVERBS 15:14

*The heart of the discerning acquires knowledge; the ears of the wise seek it out.*

PROVERBS 18:15

---

The Israelites, under their courageous captain, were full of faith, ready to take the Promised Land. These were the children of a faithless generation. They had lived in the wilderness without a city or country to call home for as long as they could remember. Forty years had elapsed since their parents had begun their wilderness wanderings due to unbelief. That generation had died out except for Joshua and Caleb. God kept these two alive because, of twelve men sent to spy out Canaan, they alone had believed God and encouraged Israel to go take the land. The others, cowering in fear and unbelief, made Israel feel like grasshoppers compared to the Canaanites. Thus Israel rebelled against God and refused to seize the land.

Here it was, forty years later. God told Joshua, "You and all these people, get ready to cross the Jordan River into the land I am about to give to them—to the Israelites. I will give you every place where you set your foot, as I promised Moses. . . . Be strong and courageous, because you will lead these people to inherit the land I swore to their forefathers to give them"( Joshua 1:2-3, 6).

Joshua was ready. He had been ready for forty years! He ordered his officers, "Go through the camp and tell the people, 'Get your supplies ready. Three days from now you will cross the Jordan here to go in and take possession of the land the LORD your God is giving you for your own'" (v. 11). His officers were ready, too. "Whatever you have commanded us we will do," they replied, "and wherever you send us we will go" (Joshua 1:16).

The obstacles that had so frightened the earlier spies had not evaporated. The region's people were still huge, the cities well-fortified. Before doing anything else, Israel would have to face the formidable city of Jericho. The first city west of the Jordan, it stood at the entrance of the mountain passes that led to the land's interior. Capturing Jericho was key to the entire campaign to take the Promised Land.

As far as Joshua knew, he would be waging a conventional battle against this heavily fortified city. Therefore he needed strategic information. From a place in Moab called Shittim, the last stopping place east of the Jordan River, he sent two spies into the land to gather facts. Only a tight circle knew of the secret mission since the last such spy mission forty years earlier had brought disaster. "Go, look over the land," he told the two, "especially Jericho."

The spies entered Jericho by mixing with the crowds going through the gate. They must have stared hard at the city's wall as they went in, for breaching this wall was the only way Israel's army could invade the city. At nightfall they stopped at Rahab's house—a house of prostitution and an inn. As a prostitute, Rahab provided lodging and favors for travelers. Hers was probably a good place for the spies to stay, since traveling merchants regularly asked directions to such establishments. Unfamiliar faces often went in and out of her house. The two could inconspicuously gather information there and, if noticed, be mistaken as Rahab's customers.

As with other Canaanite cities, Jericho's wall actually consisted of two walls spaced about fifteen feet apart with houses built between them. In that Rahab's house was such a dwelling, this was another strategic reason for the spies to go there. If necessary, they could quickly flee through her window on the wall.

Prostitution in Canaan was a business enterprise woven into the society's fabric. These agricultural communities practiced cultic prostitution, particularly related to the Canaanite fertility goddess Astarte. Both men and women dedicated their lives to the deity, performing sexual acts with worshipers to induce the deified forces of nature to follow their example. This, they believed, would assure them continued prosperity. In this society, therefore, prostitutes provided a respectable public service. Of course, Hebrew law specifically prohibited such prostitution (Deuteronomy 23:17-18).

Rahab was no detached misfit on the outer edge of society. As a smart businesswoman, she had learned to keep her eyes and ears open. In her business she probably heard a great deal. She kept abreast of the news and heard the latest gossip from her clientele. Traveling merchants told her stories about Israel. Also soldiers she had as customers probably kept her informed.

Jericho's soldiers were a brawny, fierce bunch. But despite their military bravado and the seeming impregnability of Jericho's defenses, another reality had taken shape in Rahab's heart. For the past forty years in Canaan it was commonly known how Israel's God had delivered His people from Egypt and dried up the Red Sea. All of Canaan had heard the extraordinary stories and felt fear.

Even so, the Canaanites never renounced their gods and turned to this true and living God. They believed that although He was a nature God able to part the Red Sea and a war God able to defeat other kings, He was not a fortress God able to breach their mighty walls. During the ensuing years, the true God who had so abundantly proven Himself had given the Canaanites ample opportunity to turn and repent. They had refused.

Rahab felt alarm over her sins and the sins of her people. She sensed that their time had run out, that Jericho was hopelessly vulnerable, that Israel's God was above all the gods she had ever worshiped, that He was too powerful for them. She realized He would soon send a much-deserved judgment on her country and that Israel would be His instrument. *Israel could invade anytime*, she thought, *and my house on the city wall is especially vulnerable!*

Yet while she shared the general mood of fear around her, Rahab felt something else stir her heart—hope. With a strange respect for this foreign deity and for His people, she somehow believed that He was just and that if she turned to Him, He would mercifully provide a way of salvation for her. Thus her heart told her to take courage, to go against her own people and government, and to trust herself to this God's supreme power and mercy.

Staking her life on a belief that Israel's God was the One to whom she could commit her life and future, she took in the two Israeli spies and hid them. Harboring these enemies was an extremely dangerous move for her. If the spies were discovered, the authorities would have her executed for treason. Nevertheless, her discerning heart told her that not only would the advantages outweigh the risks, but that also God was opening this door of opportunity to her.

Rumors had been circulating that Israel might be preparing to invade, and the citizens of Jericho were already nervously on alert for anything unusual. That evening someone went to the king and informed him that Israelites had come to spy out the land and that they were at Rahab's place. So the king sent Rahab an urgent message: "Bring out the men who came to you and entered your house, because they have come to spy out the whole land" (Joshua 2:3). In other words, not only was Jericho at risk but also all of Canaan.

But Rahab, having chosen her path, assured the spies she was on their side. She hid them under stalks of harvested flax she had stacked and drying on her roof. "Yes," she told the king's messengers, "the men came to me, but I did not know where they had come from. At dusk, when it was time to close the city gate, they left. I don't know which way they went." Then she strongly urged them, "Go after them quickly. You may catch up with them" (Joshua 2:4-5). So the king's men set out on the road to the Jordan River in pursuit of the spies.

While the king's men searched the countryside, Rahab went back to the rooftop to transact some business—not her usual kind though. Her discerning heart understood the criticalness of the moment. This was life-and-death business, her one opportunity to secure salvation for herself and her family. With the two men's lives in her hands, Rahab had a captive audience. They had no choice but to hear this Canaanite out.

But wasn't she a pagan idolater—and a prostitute at that? Yet God was pouring treasure into her heart, giving her a remarkable sense of His sovereignty. If these men had entered Jericho with doubts about His wanting Israel to conquer the land, Rahab, with her discerning heart, convinced them. "I know that the LORD has given this land to you," she assured them, "and that a great fear of you has fallen on us, so that all who live in this country are melting in fear because of you. We have heard how the LORD dried up the water of the Red Sea for you when you came out of Egypt, and what you did to Sihon and Og, the two kings of the Amorites east of the Jordan, whom you completely destroyed. When we heard of it, our hearts melted and everyone's courage failed because of you" (Joshua 2:9-11).

Then, renouncing her former beliefs and passionately declaring her faith in Israel's God, she said, "For the LORD your God is God in heaven above and on the earth below." Her bold confession must have shocked the men. But she was not finished. Knowing that Jericho did not stand a chance of keeping Israel outside its walls, she petitioned them, saying, "Now then, please swear to me by the LORD that you will show kindness to my family, because I have shown kindness to you. Give me a sure sign that you will spare the lives of my father and mother, my brothers and sisters, and all who belong to them, and that you will save us from death" (Joshua 2:12-13).

Owing Rahab not only their lives but the success of the entire mission, the men promised, "Our lives for your lives! If you don't tell what we are doing, we will treat you kindly and faithfully when the LORD gives us the land."

Once it was safe for the men to leave under the cover of night, Rahab let down a rope—a scarlet cord—through her window. Knowing that the hills around Jericho had many caves for hiding, she advised them as if she were herself a military strategist: "Go to the hills so the pursuers will not find you. Hide yourselves there three days until they return, and then go on your way."

Before leaving, the men warned Rahab that their oath would only be binding during the invasion if her scarlet cord hung from her window. Also her family members must be in her house if they expected to be spared. The two men would take responsibility for those inside the house but not for anyone who ran out into the street. Then they cautioned her, saying, "But if you tell what we are doing, we will be released from the oath you made us swear" (Joshua 2:20).

"Agreed," Rahab replied. "Let it be as you say." So she sent them down the scarlet rope—their means of escape and later hers—and they departed. She immediately tied the scarlet cord in the window, her sign to those outside that she believed in the God of Israel's ultimate victory.

The two men did exactly as Rahab had instructed. They stayed in the hills for three days until their pursuers returned to Jericho. Then they returned to Joshua and reported all that had transpired. Bolstered by Rahab's testimony, they confidently declared, "The LORD has surely given the whole land into our hands; all the people are melting in fear because of us" (Joshua 2:24).

Because of this faith-filled report, Joshua had Israel set out first thing the next morning toward the Jordan River. He told the people, "Consecrate yourselves, for tomorrow the LORD will do amazing things among you" (Joshua 3:5). And God did. Following the ark of the covenant carried by priests, the waters of the Jordan stopped flowing before them. All of Israel passed through the river on dry ground! After setting up a memorial of twelve stones at the river, they proceeded to make camp. Here all Israeli men were circumcised, and the people celebrated the Passover.

They had been there several days when Joshua received the plan of attack from a high-ranking angel—the "commander of the Lord's army." The armed men, divided into forward and rear battalions, must march around Jericho silently once each day for six days and then return to camp. The ark of the covenant, proceeded by seven priests constantly blowing trumpets, must be carried between the battalions. On the seventh day, they must march around the city seven times and then give a loud shout. The city's wall would collapse so they could seize the town.

While Israel was busy carrying out the battle plan, marching around the city once each day, the tension inside Jericho's walls became unbearable. All activity within the city halted. The city was shut up tighter than a drum; no one could go in or out. Atop their trusted walls, soldiers stood in frozen dread, staring at the throng of Israelites, hoping against hope that their own gods would somehow rescue them. But only in one crowded house was there reason for hope. Rahab, confident of her covenant with Israel and Israel's God, had convinced her entire family to come and find safety there. No doubt from time to time she checked her scarlet cord just to make sure it was securely in place.

Israel marched for six days without saying a word. On the seventh day, after they compassed Jericho for the seventh time that day, amid the blasting trumpets, a battle cry rang out. Joshua, with surging faith, commanded, "Shout! For the LORD has given you the city! The city and all that is in it are to be devoted to the LORD. Only Rahab the prostitute and all who are with her in her house shall be spared, because she hid the spies we sent" (Joshua 6:16-17).

Thus Israel shouted their war cry, and the mighty Jericho wall shuddered and then collapsed, evidently leaving intact Rahab's small section. All the soldiers charged in and took the city. Joshua commanded the two men who had spied out the land, "Go into the prostitute's house and bring her out and all who belong to her, in accordance with your oath to her" (v. 22).

So they brought out Rahab and her entire family. As ceremonially unclean Gentiles, the family had to stay in a place outside Israel's camp. Ultimately, however, the record says she was identified with the people of Israel: "But Joshua spared Rahab the prostitute, with her family and all who belonged to her, because she hid the men Joshua had sent as spies to Jericho—and she lives among the Israelites to this day" (v. 25).

It was no accident that the spies came to Rahab's house. God directed them to her, knowing that her heart was not only open to His truth, but that she discerned a proper response to that truth. Since the time of the historian Josephus, attempts have been made to represent Rahab as an innkeeper and not a harlot, but the Hebrew word used, along with New Testament references, confirm that she was what she was—a harlot. God planned for Rahab to play a key role in Israel's victory over Jericho. Her faith-response accomplished great things.

God uses people to accomplish His purposes no matter how seedy or insignificant their past. Rahab did not let her sinful past keep her from laying hold of the treasures of God's grace. She seized the new role God had for her among His people, and because she trusted Him, safety from His judgment was only the beginning of her rewards.

Rahab must have become a celebrated heroine in Israel because we see her blessed beyond measure in marrying into an exceedingly prominent Israeli family. Her husband Salmon was the son of Nahshon, Aaron the high priest's brother-in-law. Nahshon's sister, Elisheba, bore Aaron his four sons. Nahshon was also the leader and captain of the tribe of Judah mentioned prominently in the Old Testament.[2]

As Salmon's wife, Rahab bore Boaz who would become Ruth's husband. Most amazingly, she became ancestress to King David and is included in the lineage of Jesus Christ.[3] Rahab is one of only four women mentioned in Matthew's genealogy of Jesus Christ.

While earlier Jewish literature has little to say about Rahab, later literature often praises her beauty and sometimes even considers her a prophetess and a model convert. An utterly lost and insignificant woman enjoyed an amazing miracle of redemption and subsequent recognition among God's people. It began with a heart that discerned truth.

Rahab is included in another New Testament list—"the hall of faith"—in the book of Hebrews: "By faith the prostitute Rahab, because she welcomed the spies, was not killed with those who were disobedient" (Hebrews 11:30-31).

---

*Who is wise? He will realize these things. Who is discerning? He will understand them. The ways of the LORD are right; the righteous walk in them, but the rebellious stumble in them.*

HOSEA 14:9

---

## LESSONS FOR OUR OWN HEARTS

I was a young woman in Hollywood when God gave me a revelation. At the time I was as lost as anyone could be, believing with Nietzsche that "God is dead" and serving my own idols. Since my childhood, people had pounded into me that my life's purpose was to "get ahead"—to become rich and successful. One day I heard that Jackie Kennedy had married billionaire Aristotle Onassis (yes, it was a few years ago). *Wow!* I thought. *With a billion dollars, she can go anywhere, buy anything, do anything, be anyone she wants to be. If only that had happened to me.*

Out of nowhere a foreign and horrible thought hit me. *Cheryl, if you had everything Jackie has, you would not be one bit happier because you would still be you, and you would still have to live with yourself—and, as you know, you can't stand yourself.*

Believe it or not, this was a shattering revelation to me. I suddenly saw how everything I lived for and everything I could conceive of living for was, like fool's gold, worthless treasure. None of it could ever satisfy my aching heart. If I had all the world, I would still be miserable. Instantly my whole foundation crumbled before me. All I could think of to do was to die. I wept and wept over my utterly worthless and futile existence.

What I did not know was that God loved me and was giving me a gift—a discerning heart—to help lead me out of my worldly perception of reality into the treasures of His truth. Not too long afterward, I, like Rahab, escaped my doom and found new life in God among His people. It did not stop there though. Discernment has led me through many tangled mazes of confusion.

Oh, how we need discernment! We need it in every area of life. It is *vital* to our victory as Christians. I am not necessarily talking about a specific gift of discernment given to some of His people but about a general discernment that God wants us all to exercise, a discernment that enables us to distinguish between good and evil, right and wrong, better and best, essential and expendable, eternal and transient. We must grow in our awareness of reality—that is, God's perspective—how things are in His view.

On the surface Rahab seemed to have nothing at all going for her. She was a woman, a Gentile pagan, an openly sinful harlot living in a city slated for destruction. Yet God saw through all her problems and sins down to her heart. He saw a heart grappling for truth, seeking enlightenment, bending toward Him and the treasures of His kingdom. He granted her heart discernment. Then, mercifully wanting to see her spared from His coming judgment on her country, He sovereignly and specifically sent the spies to her, knowing she would understand and respond to His will.

---

*And this is my prayer: that your love may abound more and more in knowledge and depth of insight,* so that you may be able to discern what is best *and may be pure and blameless until the day of Christ, filled with the fruit of righteousness that comes through Jesus Christ— to the glory and praise of God.*

PHILIPPIANS 1:9-11, *emphasis added*

---

In Rahab's story we can see some key principles involving discernment. Let's take them to heart; let's learn to exercise our hearts toward godly discernment.

*We must discern the times.* If we want to navigate our way successfully through the minefields of deception in these times, it will take discernment. Like Rahab, we live in a disobedient and sinful society. Even the church, while asserting that revival is on the way, is in a time of precipitant moral decline. We have become tainted by and accustomed to abhorrent cultural values and standards. Largely, we are complacent, self-sufficient, and prayerless. While New Age spirituality is replacing secularism in our culture, much of the church has become secularized and unspiritual.

How can we interpret the great issues of our time and make any contribution to our culture apart from exercising our hearts toward godly discernment? We must be reawakened to God's truth, discerning His purposes. The Scriptures testify of His will. Yet only those who have had their understanding enlightened by His Spirit can understand them.

Can you see the signs around you? Rahab did. Her first recorded words to the spies were, "I know." She did not just *think* Israel's God was the true God, that He meant business, and that judgment was coming—she *knew* it. Her discernment enabled her to read and interpret the signs properly. She had no way of knowing exactly when Israel would strike her city, but she felt urgency in her soul.

Jesus will come soon for a people eagerly waiting for Him; those who are not prepared will be swept away in chaos. Since conflicting opinions about what He is saying and doing will only continue to proliferate, we must exercise discernment in these "perilous times."

*We must discern our need.* After properly evaluating the times, Rahab discerned her need and the need of her loved ones. She understood her desperate need for salvation. In fact, as soon as the king's messengers left her house, she ran straight to the rooftop and began her negotiations with the spies. It would not wait because she knew her life and the lives of all her loved ones hung in the balance. She made sure her opportunity would not pass her by.

Rahab was so convinced of their common need that she could convey to her entire family that the attack could come at any time. She convinced them to stay at her house. Often we act as if we think that we and our loved ones will be here forever, as if God's purpose will wait. The psalmist's prayer for discernment should be ours: "Show me, O LORD, my life's end and the number of my days; let me know how fleeting is my life" (Psalm 39:4) and "Teach us to number our days aright, that we may gain a heart of wisdom" (Psalm 90:12). Would that we all had such intense desire and motivation to secure the salvation of our family and friends!

*We must discern God's desire for us.* Somehow Rahab could "fix (her) eyes not on what is seen, but on what is unseen . . . " (2 Corinthians 4:18). She perceived that despite Jericho's long history of seeming invulnerability, God would soon grant His people victory over her own people. She knew the two men she had invited into her house had the power to save her because of the God they represented. She reached out in faith for His grace.

We might be inclined to reject someone like Rahab. Who would think she could have an interest in God? But she discerned that God had grace for her to obtain. While she had absolutely no merit to deserve His grace, He chose her, and He still chooses people just like her. Grace—God's unmerited favor—is for those with absolutely no claim to righteousness.

If you sometimes feel like an unworthy failure, remember Rahab. She was blessed, not for her lifestyle, but for her heart that discerned the truth and reached out in faith to embrace it. She knew who God was, and she knew who she was. She trusted Him to redeem her life. If God can so bless this pagan Canaanite prostitute, you can surely rise above your debilitating circumstances and trust God for victory. He is no respecter of persons. Through His blood shed on the cross, Christ has a scarlet cord of salvation for you. Not only does this assure escape from a hopeless life of defeat and rejection, but it promises entrance into a blessed life of power and victory.

---

*Who is wise? He will realize these things. Who is discerning? He will understand them. The ways of the LORD are right; the righteous walk in them, but the rebellious stumble in them.*

HOSEA 14:9

---

We must discern where to stand. Rahab discerned that she had a choice to make. She could not simply let life happen to her and see how things played themselves out in the future. Further, she discerned something that even many in Israel missed—and don't many of us miss it, too?—that the Lord is God, that she must commit her entire life to Him. She realized that she could not balance Canaanite and Israeli religion, embracing both light and darkness. She must choose her loyalty and make a firm-footed stand in her pursuit of God or do nothing at all. She must risk all she had—even her life— for this God she did not yet even know.

Other Canaanites feared, but they did not believe. They clung loyally to their gods that were no gods, and they perished with them. But Rahab refused to go along with the rest of the perishing world.

When she chose to receive Jericho's enemies, she denied everything for which her country stood. She was no longer a part of Jericho. Renouncing her past, she had a new loyalty—a higher one.

Now to some, this might seem drastic, a disloyal and treasonous betrayal of her own people. Fact is, when we are forced to decide between the one true God and our family, friends, or nation, God deserves our highest loyalty. The time comes when we must choose God or perish. Proper discernment tells us that we can never remain loyal to the gods of our culture and loyal to the true God; unity with falsehood always comes at the expense of truth.

Yet how tempted we are to try to compromise! Sometimes we feel tempted to cave in to societal pressures or sentimentality. We may have relatives who think us disloyal in our choices. They may disagree with our decision to leave a particular religion, church, or belief system; they feel betrayed. But those who bow to familial or cultural pressure and refuse to follow God's lead not only condemn themselves but those who may have followed them to God.

*We must discern what action to take.* The apostle James asks the question, "In the same way, was not even Rahab the prostitute considered righteous for what she did when she gave lodging to the spies and sent them off in a different direction?" (James 2:25). He makes the case here that believing the truth without taking appropriate action would not have saved Rahab. Everything she had discerned up to this point led her to take specific actions.

Perceiving that she must work with the spies if they would save her, she hid them. When the king's messengers came, she lied to protect them. While we would be hard pressed to justify Rahab's lying to cover her subversive activity, she had her reasons. First, in wartime situations deceiving an enemy is a normal practice. Also, as a pagan, she likely knew little of God's moral law. Finally, protecting God's people was a higher principle in her mind than honesty. With no perfect solution to her dilemma, she did the best she knew. Thus God forgave her lie because of her faith.

After Rahab courageously sent the king's messengers away, she knew exactly what to do next. She went straight to the Israeli spies, and confessing her faith in their God, secured an oath of deliverance for her and her family. She then planned the two men's escape route.

Often we, too, face difficult and confusing dilemmas for which we need discernment. Sometimes, as in Rahab's case, it is even a life-or-death matter. It is one thing to recognize our need, however, and quite another to discern the appropriate response to that need.

The apostle Paul tells us, "I keep asking that the God of our Lord Jesus Christ, the glorious Father, may give you the Spirit of wisdom and revelation, so that you may know him better. I pray also that *the eyes of your heart may be enlightened* in order that you may know the hope to which he has called you, the riches of his glorious inheritance in the saints, and his incomparably great power for us who believe . . . " (Ephesians 1:17-19, emphasis added).

Paul prays here for you! He wants you to grow in Christ; he wants you to know what is yours in Him, to have heart knowledge, not just head knowledge. This first takes opening "the eyes of your heart" so Christ can pour into it His enlightening discernment. With a discerning heart, you will be ready for a full revelation and a full realization of all the rich treasures God has for you in Christ.

## Heart Check

1. How discerning is your heart? What are some helpful ways you can grow in discernment?

2. How confident are you of God's calling and direction in your life? Have the things God has shown you made a difference in how you live and how you influence others?

3. Have you given in to any misplaced loyalties? Have you, like Rahab, put your life, your future, on the line for Christ?

4. What is the most important principle you can apply to your life from Rahab's example?

5. Compose a prayer to God in response to this chapter's lessons.

# 4

## THE SEDUCIBLE HEART

GENESIS 1:26-28; 2:18—4:26

FIRST WOMAN IN THE WORLD, final masterpiece in God's creation, mother of us all, ranking with her husband above all other creatures, made in God's own image, flawlessly beautiful—her name was Eve.

Eve walked with her husband, Adam, before God in an unspoiled and perfect paradise—crystal-clear waters, unpolluted perfumed air, lush natural beauty in every direction, happy animals of all kinds frisking together in complete harmony. Eve knew no tears, only joy. Adam adored her. Laughing, loving, working, and playing with her husband in her wondrous home, Eve was a woman complete and fulfilled in every respect.

What more could she want? Only one thing—the one thing God had denied her. Because of it, she foolishly rebelled against the One who withheld nothing she truly needed, the One who was the very source of her life and all her blessings. Satan saw in her an easy target, and she proved him correct. Falling prey to his sinister scheme, she tumbled from her pinnacle of perfection to become the world's first sinner.

We call Eve's heart The Seducible Heart. Not solidly fixed on God and His purposes, it readily went astray. Turning from faith and obedience to God, she fell into unbelief and disobedience and lost the wonderful treasures that God had prepared for her heart. We see here such irony! Rahab, who had been guilty of sin, had a discerning heart impressing her to embrace truth and reject lies; yet Eve, who had been innocent of sin, had a seducible heart impressing her to embrace lies and reject truth. Consequently Rahab received mercy, Eve condemnation.

---

*We will no longer be infants, tossed back and forth by the waves, and blown here and there by every wind of teaching and by the cunning and craftiness of men in their deceitful scheming.*

EPHESIANS 4:14

---

Before God introduced Eve, He created Adam from the dust of the ground and placed him in the Garden of Eden, a delightful paradise of breathtaking beauty, where He could lavish His love on him. With joyful new discoveries on every side, Adam had enough in the garden to fill his every appetite—aesthetic, intellectual, physical, and spiritual.

Amid picturesque trees of all descriptions were two other trees—the tree of life and the tree of the knowledge of good and evil. God told Adam, "You are free to eat from any tree in the garden; but you must not eat from the tree of the knowledge of good and evil, for when you eat of it you will surely die."

Interesting. "You are free to"; "but you must not." This double-edged sword separated Adam from every other animal. The animals, with no such capacity for moral choice, live in a state of captivity to their urges. Adam, however, was "free" to choose his course and stick by it. He could choose to be morally responsible.

After creating the whole world, God saw that "it was very good." Yet, watching carefully over Adam's needs, He noted that one thing in His creation remained "not good." Adam had "no suitable helper." God said, "It is not good for the man to be alone. I will make a helper suitable for him" (Genesis 2:18). So He put Adam into a deep sleep and took one of his ribs[1] and fashioned someone perfectly suited for him.

Why didn't God make Eve from the dust like every other creature? He wanted Adam to know that they alone shared an essential identity in "the image of God." Formed from Adam, his wife would not only be the same flesh and blood, but also of like nature and essence—endowed with reason and understanding, having similar faculties and functions. Neither could be all God intended apart from the other. Uniquely human, they would be equal partners, counterparts, complements. Together they would enjoy loving fellowship, serving their Creator with single-hearted devotion. Together they would exercise dominion over all creation and populate the earth, and together they would delight in never-ending discoveries of the boundless treasures of their God.

When God presented Eve to her husband, Adam looked at her and thought, *Wow!* He knew he was finally complete and excitedly declared, "This is now bone of my bones and flesh of my flesh; she shall be called 'woman,' for she was taken out of man." Thus the two became the first family and established the first home. Innocent, with no awareness of guilt or shame, they joyfully ran naked like children, without embarrassment.

What a wonderful life God created for Eve. She knew no difficulty, disharmony, disease, or death. Yet one day trouble came looking for her. Satan, the author of evil, came disguised as a seductive serpent to dispense his heart's vile treasure. God had hurled this mutinous angel out of heaven. Now, full of bitter hatred and armed with pride, Satan vengefully schemed to break God's heart and ruin His plan for humanity.

By spreading his rebellion to Eve and then to Adam, he could destroy the crown of creation and usurp their authority over the earth. While this crafty creature was a mere subordinate to Eve and had no power to coerce her, he was a master of subtlety. So catching her off guard when she was alone, he approached with condescending arrogance.

"Did God really say, 'You must not eat from any tree in the garden?'" he asked incredulously. In other words: "Did God really say such a silly thing as that, you naive woman?" With it he implied she could doubt God's motives, that He might not care for her as much as she thought, that He had some unfair reason for withholding something from her. This was the first time Eve had considered that she might question God, that His Word was open to her judgment.

Trying to recover, she assured the serpent that he was wrong: "We may eat fruit from the trees in the garden, but God *did* say, 'You must not eat fruit from the tree that is in the middle of the garden, and you must not touch it, or you will die.'" Still, the poison was already worming its way into her heart. Having led her to begin questioning God, he went for the kill.

"You will not surely die," he boldly railed against God's Word. In these few challenging words, he spoke volumes. It was now his word against God's, and God's Word could no longer be trusted. God's integrity, His wisdom, His penalty for disobedience were all up for debate. To contradict and reinterpret God's Word could now be justified.

Oh, Eve! If only you had fled the tempter upon hearing God's Word challenged. God created within you a will that could resist. But, alas, after the serpent landed his first successful blow, you let him come with the next, emboldening him even more.

Pitting bare assertions against the work and worth of God, he chose his next words carefully. He portrayed God as a liar possessed with jealousy and pride. He then offered disobedience as the preferred way to personal blessing and satisfaction: "For God knows that when you eat of it your eyes will be opened, and you will be like God, knowing good and evil."

Susceptible to the serpent's persuasive charm, she succumbed to doubt and disobedience. Instead of focusing on all God had given her, she obsessed over the one thing He had withheld. Rather than believing that the restrictions placed on her were for her best, she came to see God as stingy and selfish. No longer content with the pure and priceless treasures He had poured into her heart, she wanted forbidden treasure. "Humph! God wants to curtail my happiness. He intends to keep me ignorant, to restrict me from the freedom and honor I would receive by eating the fruit. If He were not holding out on me, He would *want* me to eat from this tree."

How cunningly the serpent had redirected Eve's affection and ambition away from knowing God and to "knowing good and evil." She now thought she could attain goodness beyond what God had offered, that she could suddenly rise above her wretchedly inferior state. What a terrible affront to God! What an insult to His love!

"You will be like God," the serpent contended. This was the temptation that had led to his own downfall, and Eve also found it enthralling. Lusting for this treasure, she picked up Satan's belief, consented to his theology, embraced his anti-God faith. Whether fully aware of it or not, she came to see God as a rival, an enemy to outmaneuver, one from whom she must gain independence. She would exalt herself above God, declare her independence, achieve God-ness herself.

Eve did not realize that the serpent had seduced her heart, twisted God's Word, and manipulated her emotions. Still, she was without excuse. She moved in to examine the tree's fruit more closely. Although the garden supplied a rich variety of fruit, this fruit suddenly looked most luscious, even irresistible. Feeling deprived and her heart aching with desire for divine wisdom, she wondered, "How can I ever be truly happy again if I don't partake of *this* fruit?" Craving it, her mouth watered; she could think of nothing else.

So Eve mistook the slippery slope to sin and death for a path to ultimate enlightenment and the highest heavens. Picking the fruit— her heart's new treasure—she ate it, and the mother of all the living also became the mother of all the dying.

One tragedy of yielding to sin is that its effect spreads to others. Thinking the serpent right—she did not die by eating the fruit—she proceeded to "play the devil's advocate" and enticed Adam to eat of the sumptuous fruit as well. Her sin, like an oil spill, spread to Adam and from him to the entire human race. Adam and Eve did not suffer death immediately, but they did set the dying process in motion. Worse than the physical dying, however, was the spiritual death of separation from God. The vacuum left by forfeiting their relationship with God would bring unutterable pain.

The eyes of the guilty pair indeed "opened." Just as the serpent promised, Eve became "as God, knowing good and evil." But she had been given only a half-truth. While she would come to know evil, be evil, and live with evil, she would never ascend to godhood. Though she was created in God's image, that image became severely tarnished, and the Godlikeness she aspired to became devil-likeness instead.

Now choked with wicked treasure, the hearts of Eve and Adam condemned them. They felt ashamed for their physical nakedness, to be sure. But more than that, their outer nakedness only mirrored the inner shame of having the innocence stripped from their souls. Their relationship with God ruptured, they wanted to hide, and they sought to cover themselves and their sin with fig leaves. What made them think they could hide from the all-seeing, all-knowing God?

Suddenly they heard Him coming. "Where are you?" He called. Of course, God knew where Adam and Eve were hiding, but He gave Adam an opportunity to acknowledge his sin.

Adam did not. Instead, trying to explain it away, he said, "I heard you in the garden, and I was afraid because I was naked; so I hid."

"Who told you that you were naked?" God asked. "Have you eaten from the tree from which I commanded you not to eat?"

Not only did the two try to hide their bodies under fig leaves; they tried to hide their sin under excuses. Adam replied, "The woman you put here with me—she gave me some fruit from the tree, and I ate it." In this, not only did Adam blame Eve, but he blasphemously transferred his guilt to God for giving him Eve to make him fall. In essence he said, "If you hadn't given me this woman, God, I wouldn't have gotten into trouble!"

"What is this you have done?" God asked Eve. Seeking to exonerate herself rather than owning up to her sin, she likewise pointed her finger elsewhere, saying, "The serpent deceived me, and I ate." True, he had tempted her, but she chose to sin.

Neither of the guilty pair acknowledged personal guilt but chose to plead innocent, justifying themselves. God reacted to their sin in a manner consistent with His perfect moral nature. With breaking heart, He exacted divine justice upon the three guilty parties. He consigned the serpent to crawl on his belly and eat dust all his life. Eve would endure multiplied pain in childbirth, and her husband would rule over her. Adam must engage in sweaty toil to get food from ground cursed because of him. Also, when he died—for now he must—he would return to the dust from which he came.

After pronouncing judgment, God graciously made garments for Adam and Eve and clothed them. He then sent them away from their garden paradise, out to a world of thorns, thistles, and heartache. Placing a cherubim with a flaming sword to bar their way back, He made certain they would never return to eat of the tree of life and live forever.

Why did God allow this human tragedy? Couldn't He have stepped in to avert disaster by stopping the serpent from tempting Eve? Yes, but this was a test He allowed. He knew he could demand obedience—but never love. He created our first parents in His image, with the power of moral choice. Unlike the animals, their temptation was not beyond their ability to withstand. They could choose to love and obey God, or they could choose to spurn Him and go their own way.

God put the tree within the first couple's reach so they could deliberately choose to refuse temptation and walk voluntarily with Him. Without this power of choice, they would be either like programmed robots or prisoners of forced obedience. Their response would be without love and volition, and therefore meaningless. Thus, the two special trees in the garden provided an exercise in choice with blessings for obedience (the tree of life) and punishment for disobedience (the tree of the knowledge of good and evil). God wanted Adam and Eve to choose love and loyalty to Him.

Eve's and Adam's trespass was so serious that it set in motion the entire human race's disposition for sin and alienation from God. Eve saw the tragic consequences of sin in her offspring when her son Cain jealously murdered his brother Abel. Here she adds to her list of firsts—"first mourner." Humanity has had reason to mourn ever since.

If only Eve had been content to eat from the tree of life! What she threw away by eating from the other tree! Life in the Garden of Eden was perfect, just like living in heaven! While she *could* sin if she wanted, she had no reason *to* sin. God supplied her every need. She had it all—a perfect life, perfect husband, perfect environment, and perfect fellowship with the perfect God. If Eve had not given in to temptation, she would have remained an immortal creature living in paradise forever. But doubting God's Word and His love, she yielded her heart to Satan and became the prototype for all sinners.

How could any woman know the anguish Eve suffered for her sin? What must it be like to see the perfect image of God in your life forever marred, to realize you sinned against the greatest mercy and the dearest and most pure of loves? What was it like to move from perfect fellowship in utopian Eden to an existence where, because of you, sin is introduced to humanity, the earth is cursed, you are banned from your paradise, and disease, pain, and death become the norm?

In this story of original sin, we find in seed form all the sin and passion that will for all time ravage human society. Paradise is lost, and the entire world comes under a curse. Eve, who was equal in Eden, was now ruled by her husband; the "battle of the sexes" is on. No human will ever live in innocent bliss again. For human nature lodged in our first parents has passed to all their children. A corrupted and fallen race, all creation groans because of them. It began with a seducible heart.

Even though God banned our first parents from the garden, He did not leave them without hope. His justice was punitive, but it was also redemptive. A world of lost and ruined sinners would come from Eve, but so also would the Redeemer. This One would right the wrong, undo the curse, and bring hope, joy, and salvation to all who would receive Him.

After cursing the serpent, God added, "I will put enmity between you and the woman, and between your offspring and hers; he will crush your head, and you will strike his heel." He was speaking of the cosmic battle between Satan and Christ. God would send Christ the Redeemer to crush Satan's kingdom. Christ would suffer and die but rise victoriously from the dead, wresting Satan's grip off of humanity. In that day He would atone for Eve's sin, and just as God had given her animal skins to cover her nakedness, He would provide humanity with robes of righteousness to cover their sin. Paradise lost would become paradise regained. For "mercy triumphs over judgment!"[2]

## LESSONS FOR OUR HEARTS

Don't we consistently prove ourselves Eve's children by repeating her mistakes? Again and again Satan strolls up and, arousing our desires, entices us to doubt God's Word and move away from the way of life to which God calls us. And how do we respond? Too often by complying. Easily seduced and manipulated, we shift our focus from what God has given us to what He has withheld. Rationalizing and justifying ourselves all the way, our hearts become inflamed with rebellion and ingratitude toward Him.

Shelley and Tim were our good friends. We had lots in common. Tim and my husband, Clay, met in seminary and graduated together. We were young, loved Jesus, and had joyfully dedicated our lives to serving Him. We laughed, cried, and prayed together. Once, when we had gone through a devastating experience, we desperately needed God's direction. Shelley, like the mouthpiece of God, spoke the exact words we needed to hear. So profound were her words that we knew they were directly from God. He used Shelley powerfully to renew our hope for the future. While we went on to serve in the church, Tim became a military chaplain. Tim and Shelley eventually were stationed overseas in Europe.

Unfortunately Shelley didn't adjust well to her new environment, and the marriage began to show signs of strain. She became lonely and disillusioned. Satan knew her weakness, and with her heart in a vulnerable, frustrated, and seducible place, he enticed her. For an outlet Shelley began taking university classes. Her heart began to shed its good treasure as these classes influenced her to view her husband and men in general with suspicion. She began to doubt God and His plan for her life. "Eat the fruit," Satan tempted her. "You don't need your husband; you don't need God. You can write your own rules." Captivated, she soon ate. Pulling away from God and family, she began a lifestyle of drinking and partying. Shelley left Tim, and the last time we had contact with her, she was broken and lost.

Surely this story will not seem strange to many of you. You have watched helplessly as the devil destroyed lives, homes, and churches through his persuasions. Satan hates God's children; he studies us; he knows our weaknesses; he wants to steal from our hearts the precious treasures of our faith. Yes, he still entices us to indulge in what God has forbidden, provoking us to cast off restraint so he can conscript us into slavery to his evil ways. He baits his hook for us with his most effective customized bait. For the unwary, the enchantment is nearly impossible to resist.

Choosing to eat a piece of fruit may not have seemed a momentous decision to Eve. How wrong she was! As Eve's sin was serious, so is ours—so serious that Christ had to suffer intolerable agony on the cross to pay the penalty. Still, Satan constantly looks for opportunities to pull us out of God's grace and into our own sinful path. His great aspiration is to seduce God's people into ruinously falling away, "crucifying the Son of God all over again and subjecting him to public disgrace" (Hebrews 6:6).

Satan, a master of cunning, strives to incite our hearts to rebellion, to separate us from our source of life and enslave us to himself. Since the serpent so ably seduced our first mother—"it was the woman who was deceived . . . " (1 Timothy 2:14)—it behooves us to think soberly about our own vulnerability. We must take heed if we, unlike Eve, would avoid Satan's seduction. Dissecting his approach, we find the following primeval yet ever-effective techniques:

*He questions God.* "Did God *really* say . . . ?" The serpent set Eve up to wonder whether the forbidden fruit was really forbidden at all. How often do we fall into questioning whether or not something is really a sin? Why do we second-guess God? Perhaps because the tempter is knocking on our heart's door.

*He contradicts God.* "You will *not* surely die." By denying the veracity of God's Word, he wants her to deny God. If Eve thinks she knows better than God, she will doubt the danger and disobey Him. Sly serpent that he is, he tricked Eve with half-truths. Many voices around us and even in us oppose God's absolute truth with contradictory half-truths.

*He reduces God.* "For God knows that when you eat of it your eyes will be opened . . ." By making God seem small-minded and unfair, Satan seeks to reduce God in Eve's eyes. If she no longer reveres her Maker, she won't desire to honor Him, nor will she be inclined to obey Him. How foolish we are when we act as God's judge and look suspiciously at His purpose for our lives.

*He exalts the creature.* " . . . and you will be like God . . ." In reducing God, we naturally exalt ourselves. Satan dangled the fabricated carrot of "goddesshood." How amazing that we could imagine we know better how to chart our course than does our omniscient Creator! One hugely successful cult group's slogan embraced by its millions of members should not surprise us: "As man is, God once was; as God is, man may become."

Satan caught Eve's seducible heart on his line. How did she fall? Let's look at the steps and beware:

*She listened.* Eve would have been hard pressed to prevent Satan's initial approach, but she did not need to give him ground by listening to him. She did not need to let him deceive her. She should have guarded her heart's treasure. She could have consulted God when she heard His Word questioned; she could have consulted Adam. She should have known at once that nothing good would come from this conversation. If only she had declared, "Yes, I am sure God said it; I am glad He said it. I trust Him in it, and by His grace I choose to abide by it, so go away!" Her conference with Satan instead ended in disaster.

*She saw.* "When the woman saw that the fruit of the tree . . ." What did she see in this fruit? Plenty. First, she saw that it was "good for food." It appealed to her physical need. Next, she saw it was "pleasing to the eye." It appealed to her emotionally; it dazzled her sensually, not looking at all distasteful. Finally, she saw it was "desirable for gaining wisdom." It appealed to her mentally and spiritually—the most powerful temptation stirring her desire for knowledge and insight. The sight of the fruit even inflamed her ambition to transcend herself and gain the wisdom that belonged only to God. Rather than turning away, she stared at the forbidden fruit. Once she stared, she coveted.

*She took.* "she took some . . ." Eve bit in her heart before she bit with her mouth. Once her mouth began to salivate, she could little resist her temptation. Satan tempted, but she is the one who reached out and took the forbidden fruit in direct disobedience to God's Word.

*She ate.* "and ate it." This would be Eve's final picnic in paradise. She may not have intended to take when she looked or eat when she took, but the progression, once begun, led to her complete downfall. The direction of sin is always downward. Stopping it at the beginning might have been easy but not once it got rolling.

Just look at the results Eve's seducible heart wrought:

*She spread her guilt.* "She also gave some to her husband . . ." Here we see the powerful effect of sin. No sooner did Eve become a sinner than, like Satan, she became a tempter. The spirit of seduction never keeps to itself, for a "little yeast works through the whole batch of dough" (Galatians 5:9).

*She hid.* "and they hid from the Lord God . . ." God gave Eve the capacity to know and relate to Him personally. But when she and Adam violated that special relationship, they became alienated and hid from Him. Their sin also perverted their relationship with each other. They hid from each other by covering themselves with fig leaves.

*She blamed.* "The serpent deceived me . . ." The sin Eve and Adam committed together pulled them apart. Adam quickly blamed Eve for his guilt. Taking the cue, she blamed the serpent. She should have confessed her sin. She was guilty—she could not even claim the "dysfunctional home" defense!—and her excuses would never wash with God.

*She suffered the consequences.* "I will greatly increase your pains in childbearing . . . your husband . . . will rule over you." Eve's fall ruined her perfect life. She would know physical pain, and her marriage relationship would never be the same. Not only that, but she would die—"For the wages of sin is death" (Romans 6:23)—and never see her lovely garden paradise again.

We know that Satan's seductions and seducers are going "from bad to worse, deceiving and being deceived" (2 Timothy 3:13). So how can we avoid Eve's vulnerability to a seducible heart?

*Be wise, not ignorant of Satan's evil schemes.* The devil is never more dangerous than when he comes disguised as the one who cares, the earnest friend, wishing nothing but our welfare. And, oh, how he sugarcoats sin. He convinced Eve that the forbidden fruit could unlock her hidden potential. If we are not wise and alert, he can easily convince us that true freedom lies in his warped and worldly logic. Paul, emphasizing that the church must not let the devil outwit us, says, "We are not unaware of his schemes" (2 Corinthians 2:11).

---

*But I am afraid that just as Eve was deceived by the serpent's cunning, your minds may somehow be led astray from your sincere and pure devotion to Christ. For if someone comes to you and preaches a Jesus other than the Jesus we preached, or if you receive a different spirit from the one you received, or a different gospel from the one you accepted, you put up with it easily enough.*

2 CORINTHIANS 11:3-4

---

*Believe God's Word, not Satan's lies.* Failing to understand God's reasons for certain commands can lead to trouble if we have not resolved the question of our allegiance. By distorting, perverting, and confusing the truth; by twisting the Scriptures; by causing us to doubt, Satan can convince us that great gain comes from indulging in what God has forbidden. Once you believe God's Word can have error, that God does not mean what He says, that you care more about your needs than God does, you invite seduction and open the way for rebellion. Like Eve, you have accepted Satan's point of view.

Instead, exercise your freedom of choice by refusing to doubt God's Word. If we trust Him, we will obey Him whether we entirely understand His purpose or not. We will not be seducible if we hold to His Word. We must renounce all doubt, unbelief, and disloyalty toward it.

*Learn to listen to the Holy Spirit's voice, not to Satan's.* Satan wants to confuse us. He addresses us as he did Eve, calling us to question our contentment in Christ. Whispering in our ear, he asks, "Did God really say . . ."; "You're not really happy, are you?" "If God withholds _____ from you, how can you be happy?" (You can fill in the blank.) And his tactic works, doesn't it?

Jesus said, "My sheep listen to my voice; I know them, and they follow me" (John 10:27). He speaks by the Holy Spirit within us. He promised, "And I will ask the Father, and he will give you another Counselor to be with you forever—the Spirit of truth" (John 14:16-17). Practice listening to His voice.

*Look away from, not at, the object of your temptation.* We often lose the battle with the first glance of our eyes. Satan smashes through these windows of our souls with his fiery darts, penetrating and poisoning our hearts. We must, therefore, resolve in our hearts to "draw the blinds" quickly, not even peeking at the "forbidden fruit." The object of Eve's desire was not ugly. Attractive temptations are the hardest to resist. Stand instead with righteous Job who claimed, "I made a covenant with my eyes not to look lustfully . . ." and "my heart has [not] been led by my eyes" (Job 31:1, 7).

*Yield to God, not to your own desires.* Satan influences us to pit our will against God's and act independently of Him. The tempter makes us feel deprived and discontented with our life. In preferring things that God does not see fit to give us, we show contempt for the blessings He *has* given us. Eve, in the midst of incredible opulence, felt deprived, and Satan, with all of his glory in God's perfect heaven, felt deprived. We in the Western world who have so much still feel deprived unless we can have more.

Satan also appeals to our pride and ambition. The root sin of Satan, and of sinful human nature, is self-aggrandizement, the desire to exalt ourselves above God. Becoming our own authority, we decide for ourselves what is best for our lives. Self-exaltation always leads to rebellion against God. If you want victory, you must humbly and habitually yield your heart to God.

*When you sin, confess it and repent immediately.* Sin is deceitful. Those sinful "little" decisions we make today can affect our destinies. Whenever we seek to justify our sins rather than repent, we put our own fig leafs over our hearts. We are guilty, nonetheless, and our sin has created a barrier between us and God. Be sure to keep your heart open to Christ's cleansing power. In the words of James, "Confess your sins to each other and pray for each other so that you may be healed" (James 5:16). "Lone rangers" in Christ's church have already been seduced. Victory depends on healthy and accountable relationships with other believers.

*Command Satan to go.* We do not have to yield to sin. Christ has given us authority over satanic temptations. His Word promises, "Resist the devil, and he will flee from you" (James 4:7). This verse does not mean that resisting him once will bring automatic victory. We must keep on resisting. Satan came to Jesus three recorded times in the desert, landing his punches where he thought Jesus was weakest. What did Jesus do? Refusing to let Satan play with His mind through carrying on lengthy conversations, He used Scripture and rebuked the tempter: "Away from me, Satan! For it is written . . ." (Matthew 4:10). Christ's victory on the cross won victory for us over all the enemy's power and schemes. By steadfastly appropriating His victory, you guard your heart from becoming seducible.

Remember the Holy Spirit's warning concerning seducible hearts in these end times: "The Spirit clearly says that in later times some will abandon the faith and follow deceiving spirits and things taught by demons" (1 Timothy 4:1). But also take heart by remembering the complete restoration from the Fall that He promises those who remain faithful: "He who has an ear, let him hear what the Spirit says to the churches. To him who overcomes, I will give the

right to eat from the tree of life, which is in the paradise of God"
(Revelation 2:7).

## Heart Check

1. As you consider the legacies that Rahab and Eve left for their
loved ones, how can you exercise your heart to ensure that you leave
a godly legacy?

2. Those who would avoid eating forbidden fruit must not come
near the tree that bears it. Is there "forbidden fruit" that entices you
to act independently of God? How can you better avoid the path of
temptation?

3. Do you have someone to whom you are spiritually accountable, to whom you can go when you need to confess sin and receive
prayer?

4. What is the most important principle you can apply to your life
from Eve's example?

5. Compose a prayer to God in response to this chapter's lessons.

# 5

## *Ruth*

### THE FLEXIBLE HEART

RUTH, MATTHEW 1:5

WHO HAS NEVER HEARD SOME flippant mother-in-law joke? In the book of Ruth, however, we find a beautiful in-law relationship between two women. Ruth would go to any length for her mother-in-law Naomi. Orpah, Naomi's other daughter-in-law, loved her too, but she exits the story early, unable to press forward into God's purposes.

Ruth, on the other hand, refused to collapse under her circumstances. She pushed through to see her life changed and, with it, all of history as well. Ranking high on the Bible's "Who's Who" list, Ruth is one of only two women who has a book of the Bible named for her.

What made Ruth so memorable? I believe it was her heart. Hers we will call The Flexible Heart. No matter what the difficulty, this heart stays very responsive to God, enabling Him to bend and shape it for His purposes and to prepare it for His treasures. Soft and malleable, it bends with the pressures exerted upon it, thus suffering no lasting damage. When life dealt Ruth bitter blows, she adjusted herself not only to maneuver through them but to triumph over them. God loves the flexible heart. Though at times His ways may seem senseless and unfair, this heart follows His lead and yields to His will.

*I know what it is to be in need, and I know what it is to have plenty.
I have learned the secret of being content in any and every situation,
whether well fed or hungry, whether living in plenty or in want. I can
do everything through him who gives me strength.*

PHILIPPIANS 4:12-13

The story of Ruth opens "in the days when the judges ruled."
This 325-year period was Israel's Dark Age. Society was falling
apart, and "everyone did as he saw fit" (Judges 17:6). The nation
underwent the same cycle repeatedly. They sinned against God;
they came under oppression; they repented and called out to God;
God sent a deliverer to rescue them; they became complacent and
sinned again.

A severe famine came upon Israel during this period, and a
Hebrew named Elimelech took his wife, Naomi, and two sons,
Kilion and Mahlon, out of Israel about fifty miles into the neighbor-
ing country of Moab for refuge. But life in Moab went from bad to
worse. First Elimelech died. Then both sons married Moabite
women—Orpah and Ruth. Although God did not forbid marriage
with Moabites (as descendants of Lot, they were considered distant
relatives), such marriages were still frowned upon. Moabites worshiped idols. They had also refused to let the Israelites pass through
their land during the Exodus from Egypt, and they had oppressed
Israel during the time of the Judges.

Despite their national and religious differences, the family
became close-knit and loving. In time, however, more tragedy struck.
Both Kilion and Mahlon died, leaving Naomi childless and Orpah
and Ruth as childless widows. These three women suffering the des-
olation of widowhood together had no means of support and no hope
for finding any. They did have a lot of love for each other, but love
could not feed them.

Seeing nothing but biting poverty ahead, Naomi felt bitter
toward God. Rather than stay in Moab, she decided to go home. The
famine had ended, and she had no ties in Moab, so she left for Israel

with her daughters-in-law. After setting out, however, she was stricken with hopelessness. She could see only a dismal future for the two young women in Israel. "Go back, each of you, to your mother's home," she pled. "May the LORD grant that each of you will find rest in the home of another husband" (Ruth 1:8-9).

Orpah and Ruth embraced Naomi, kissing her and sobbing their hearts out. While they were not obligated to do so, both assured her they would never abandon her. "We will go back with you to your people," they promised. But Naomi thought they just didn't get it. "Return home, my daughters," she implored. "Why would you come with me? Am I going to have any more sons, who could become your husbands? Return home, my daughters" (Ruth 1:11-12). In wishing she could have more sons, she alluded to the principle of levirate marriage, a legal obligation of a dead man's brother to marry his widow. Since there were no living brothers and Naomi could have no more sons, she saw their best hope closed to them.

"The LORD's hand has gone out against me!" Naomi lamented. Orpah's heart caved in. Emotionally wrenching though it was, Naomi's logic made sense. Going on to who knows what would cost too much; another radical transition would be too painful; a life in Israel promised nothing. Orpah's family in Moab, on the other hand, would take her in. She could still make a life for herself there, get another husband, and have children. Yes, hope and security lay behind, not ahead. So Orpah yielded, and as they wept together, she kissed Naomi one last time. Then she left—and faded into obscurity.

Ruth, however, was another story; she had treasure in her heart that made her disregard Naomi's logic. Although childlessness was the worst fate to befall women in their culture, her heart refused to consider her own need. The future meant nothing if she could not fulfill her duty to the one who had been her mother for over ten years. A woman of less character could think, *I might marry again, and my late husband's mother will be in the way; she will be a burden; I don't want to support her.* Yet Ruth clung to Naomi, refusing to let her go on without her.

Naomi tried to reason with her. "Look, your sister-in-law is going back to her people and her gods. Go back with her." This reveals all that Orpah's decision meant. Not only did she leave Naomi, but she left Naomi's God; not only did she return to her people but to Chemosh, Moab's chief god. Ruth's heart, however, reached toward the God of Israel of whom she had learned from her husband and Naomi. She wanted no part of going back to Chemosh or any other god of Moab. She now believed in the true God. She would forsake neither Naomi nor the Lord.

Ruth's response to Naomi, in addition to providing some of the most beautiful and inspiring words in all the Bible, also discloses the richness of her heart's treasure. Through blinding tears, she declared her allegiance: "Don't urge me to leave you or to turn back from you. Where you go I will go, and where you stay I will stay. Your people will be my people and your God my God. Where you die I will die, and there I will be buried." Then, binding herself by an oath to stand by Naomi till death, she testified, "May the LORD deal with me, be it ever so severely, if anything but death separates you and me" (Ruth 1:15-17).

Naomi gave up trying to reason with Ruth. Henceforth, the Hebrews would be Ruth's people, and their God would be her God. The two widows journeyed on to Bethlehem together. Upon their arrival in Bethlehem, Naomi, filled with sorrow, told her former acquaintances, "Don't call me Naomi [meaning "pleasant"]. Call me Mara [meaning "bitter"] because the Almighty has made my life very bitter. I went away full, but the LORD has brought me back empty" (Ruth 1:20-21).

Ruth stood by silently as people gathered around Naomi. If she shed a tear, we never see it. In fact, she did not bemoan her lot in life at all; nor did she complain against God. Rather it seems she quietly yielded to the will of God.

Not one to idly sit back and wait for a handout from the community, Ruth was intent on adjusting to her new culture. Her flexible heart surveyed her new situation to see how she might best overcome her disadvantages. While Naomi saw nothing but problems, Ruth sought for possibilities.

It so happened that this was the time of the spring barley harvest, and Ruth saw harvesters coming from the fields outside Bethlehem carrying golden bundles of grain. She learned of the Israeli law that forbade landowners from harvesting the corners of their fields. The law also allowed gleaners—poor folk who needed food—to follow the harvesters and pick up any grain they dropped.[1]

Seeing a way for Naomi and her to survive, she probably thought, *What timing! God has led us to Bethlehem at a time when I can glean in those fields.* To one with a less flexible heart, this work might have seemed menial and degrading. True, it was undignified, but Ruth had no pride to protect, no shame to cover. Instead she saw a blessing. Turning to Naomi, she said, "Let me go to the fields and pick up the leftover grain behind anyone in whose eyes I find favor." Naomi approved.

So early in the morning, Ruth went out to a barley field and asked the foreman of the harvesters if she could glean. He granted her permission, and she started right in, determined to work her hardest so she could encourage Naomi with a good supply of grain. Men cut the grain with a sickle, and women went behind them binding the sheaves. Ruth followed the women, picking up any leftovers.

The field Ruth happened to be working belonged to a wealthy landowner named Boaz—a member of Naomi's husband's clan. Ruth had gleaned for part of the day when Boaz came to visit his field. After exchanging salutations with his field workers, Ruth caught his eye. He asked about her, and his foreman explained, "She is the Moabitess who came back from Moab with Naomi." He went on to tell how she had asked permission to glean and had worked steadily, except for a short break, from early in the morning.

Obviously the entire town, including Boaz, had heard about the tragic plight of Naomi and Ruth. And Boaz had also heard of Ruth's sacrifices for Naomi. Now, witnessing her industriousness, he was deeply impressed and went at once to talk with her. An older man with a warm expression on his face, Boaz said, "My daughter, listen to me. Don't go and glean in another field. . . . Stay here with my servant girls." He had given orders to his men not to touch her and told her that she could drink from their water jars whenever she was thirsty.

Ruth, viewing herself as little more than a beggar, knelt before Boaz and exclaimed, "Why have I found such favor in your eyes that you notice me—a foreigner?" Little did she realize that by now her loving sacrifice had already become a witness to the entire community.

Boaz told Ruth that he had heard of all she had done for Naomi and how, after her husband's death, she had left her own kindred and country to come live among strangers. He then blessed her, saying, "May the LORD repay you for what you have done. May you be richly rewarded by the LORD, the God of Israel, under whose wings you have come to take refuge."

What an awesome blessing; what a kind man; what a wonderful God! Ruth wondered how so much good could come to her in one short day. "May I continue to find favor in your eyes, my lord," she humbly responded. "You have given me comfort and have spoken kindly to your servant—though I do not have the standing of one of your servant girls" (Ruth 2:2-13).

After several more hours of labor, the harvesters stopped to eat. Ruth kept her distance, knowing her place. But Boaz invited her to come eat with them and made sure she had plenty. After that, she went back to work. What was left for gleaners was typically meager at best, so Boaz ordered his men to make Ruth's task easy by pulling stalks from their bundles and leaving them for her to find. He also told them to speak kindly to her. Ruth worked hard until evening and then threshed her barley. It came to about a bushel weighing around fifty pounds.

She excitedly carried her load back to town and brought it to Naomi, along with some leftovers from the meal. Naomi knew gleaners could not normally get this much grain. Shaken from her despondency, she exclaimed, "Blessed be the man who took notice of you!" She then asked whose field Ruth had worked in.

"The name of the man I worked with today is Boaz," Ruth replied.

Now Naomi got really excited. "The LORD bless him!" she cried. "That man is our close relative; he is one of our kinsman-redeemers" (Ruth 2:19-20).

A kinsman-redeemer was a relative who was willing to take the part of next of kin for his deceased brother. Under the law, a widow with no children had the right to this levirate marriage. The deceased husband's wife could marry his brother, and their first child would continue the deceased man's family line so that his name would not be forgotten, and his family's ownership of land would be perpetuated.[2] Because Naomi had no more sons, the nearest relative could step in and fulfill the responsibility, if he agreed.

"What might God be doing?" Naomi wondered. She urged Ruth to accept Boaz's invitation. Gleaning fields could be dangerous for a young woman, and she would be safe in his field. So Ruth did as Naomi said, availing herself of the protection of working in Boaz's field and staying close to his servant girls.

Naomi realized that Ruth's gleaning was no more than a short-term provision for them. The season would end, leaving them with no livelihood. Besides, this was no way for Ruth to live. Naomi had been praying for a solution, and now everything pointed to Boaz.

Meanwhile, Ruth worked diligently day by day in the hot sun. She worked faithfully, tirelessly, and gratefully. She sought no honor, but somehow it found her. All over town people knew of the hard-working foreigner who cared so well for her mother-in-law. She demanded nothing for herself and never complained. Transforming her lowly task into one of dignity, the young Moabitess inspired them all and won their hearts.

One day Naomi approached Ruth with a plan. "My daughter," she asked, "should I not try to find a home for you, where you will be well provided for?" Reminding Ruth that Boaz was their kinsman-redeemer, she probably told her to dress up, put on some perfume, and go on over to the threshing floor where Boaz would be winnowing barley that night. Ruth should hide herself until he finished his dinner and went to sleep. Then she should lie down at his feet and uncover them. Probably seeing Ruth's puzzled look, she added with a sparkle in her eye, "He will tell you what to do."

Ruth probably considered Naomi's instructions unusual. "What a strange custom this is! Why would Boaz know what to do?" she no doubt wondered. While parents arranged marriages, and Naomi appropriately took the initiative, one with a less flexible heart than Ruth's might have balked. Boaz was an older man, well past his prime, and tradition says Ruth was a lovely woman. She might well have gone her own way, choosing to look for a younger, more dashing man.

Yet Ruth's heart is flexible, and once again she adjusts her life to satisfy God's will. "I will do whatever you say," she answered Naomi. God looked upon this special heart with great favor. Events would quickly fall into place to change her life forever.

She went bravely to the threshing floor, and, sure enough, Boaz did as Naomi had predicted. This was the climax of the harvest season, and, working late to winnow his grain, he stayed for the night to protect it from possible theft. Once he was asleep, Ruth did exactly as Naomi had instructed her. Uncovering Boaz's feet, she lay down. She knew he would eventually wake up to cover his feet again and then notice her. Later that night, he did awaken to find her lying there. Startled, he asked, "Who are you?"

"I am your servant Ruth," she replied. "Spread the corner of your garment over me, since you are a kinsman-redeemer." Customarily a Jewish husband covered his bride with the end of his prayer shawl to signify that she had come under his protection. Thus Ruth was asking Boaz, as kinsman-redeemer, to either marry her himself or to find another man to be her husband.

It seems from his response that Boaz had already considered this possibility. He felt honored. "The LORD bless you, my daughter," he replied. "This kindness is greater than that which you showed earlier: You have not run after the younger men, whether rich or poor." Then he assured her, "And now, my daughter, don't be afraid. I will do for you all you ask. All my fellow townsmen know that you are a woman of noble character" (Ruth 3:9-11).

He was certain no one would object to Ruth, but he did see one little hitch. He was not their closest relative; another man was a nearer kinsman-redeemer. He promised to find this man in the morning and see if he were willing to do the honors. If not, he vowed, "as surely as the LORD lives I will do it." At the first blush of dawn before anyone saw her, Ruth went home.

Naomi told Ruth not to worry. She knew Boaz would not rest until he settled the matter. Sure enough, Boaz went right down to the city gate and waited till the other kinsman-redeemer came by. Calling him and the city officials together for a meeting, he carefully presented his case to the relative, saying that property now up for sale was still in Elimelech's name. As nearest relative, the man had the first option to purchase it. The man agreed to the proposal until he heard that Ruth came with the property. Realizing that marrying Ruth would be a losing proposition for him, he backed away. Buying the field would come with a duty to raise up an heir for Elimelech. Their first son would be Elimelech's, and the field would revert to that child. Therefore, his own sons would not inherit what he had bought. He would also have another family to provide for. "You redeem it yourself; I cannot do it," he said. With that, he removed his shoe, a customary symbolic act of transferring property rights to another.

With the way now cleared, Boaz announced his intent to buy the field, marry Ruth, and carry out his duties to Elimelech's family. He proclaimed, "Today you are witnesses that I have bought from Naomi all the property of Elimelech, Kilion and Mahlon. I have also acquired Ruth the Moabitess, Mahlon's widow, as my wife, in order to maintain the name of the dead with his property, so that his name will not disappear from among his family or from the town records." Punctuating the finality of this transaction, he declared again, "Today you are witnesses!" (Ruth 4:6-10).

How did the officials and townsfolk respond? They happily announced, "We are witnesses." Then they blessed Boaz, saying, "May the LORD make the woman who is coming into your home like Rachel and Leah, who together built up the house of Israel. May you have standing in Ephrathah and be famous in Bethlehem. Through the offspring the LORD gives you by this young woman, may your family be like that of Perez, whom Tamar bore to Judah."

Ruth and Boaz married, and they did have a son. The celebration that followed expresses more than joy over his birth, however; the women also rejoiced over Ruth, his mother. To Naomi, they joyfully said, "Praise be to the LORD, who this day has not left you without a kinsman-redeemer. May he become famous throughout Israel! He will renew your life and sustain you in your old age. For your daughter-in-law, who loves you and who is better to you than seven sons, has given him birth" (Ruth 4:11-15). What restoration!

The return of Naomi and Ruth to Bethlehem was clearly part of God's plan. Ruth and Boaz named their son Obed, a shortened form of Obadiah, which means "servant of the Lord." Obed became the father of Jesse, and Jesse was the father of David, king of Israel. The book of Matthew traces this lineage further, saying, " . . . and Jesse the father of King David. . . . and Jacob the father of Joseph, the husband of Mary, of whom was born Jesus, who is called Christ" (Matthew 1:6, 16).

Imagine that! This young Moabitess, called by God's grace and sovereign plan, was an ancestor of our Lord Jesus Christ! In reference to David the shepherd boy, God would say, "Man looks at the outward appearance, but the LORD looks at the heart" (1 Samuel 16:7). If true of David, so also is it true of his great-grandmother Ruth.

The young, impoverished Gentile widow came to Israel an outsider with no prospects for the future. But while her hands were empty, her heart was full of treasure. Seeing the beauty of her flexible heart, God stopped at nothing to honor and bless her. Ruth became a dedicated worshiper of the true God, and He accepted her worship. He blessed her and made her fruitful among His people. He lifted her from poverty to wealth and from obscurity to a place of honor and significance. Ruth left an endearing legacy, not only for her generation but for all that followed. God even elevated Ruth to the highly honored place of being in the lineage of kings and princes, and of the Savior of the world Himself. Through Him especially this lovely Moabitess has touched the entire world.

## LESSONS FOR OUR OWN HEARTS

Ruth's story is set in Bethlehem's barley fields at harvest time. We see workers wading through the soft straw, busily cutting, gathering, and bundling in a rich yield to take to the threshing floor. Everyone is thinking grain; no one is thinking soil. Yet beneath those golden waves of grain lay the soil. Before they could have hoped for a crop, they had to plow and cultivate that soil. The harvest was completely dependent on the soil's condition.

---

*"A farmer went out to sow his seed. As he was scattering the seed, some fell . . . on good soil, where it produced a crop—a hundred, sixty or thirty times what was sown. He who has ears, let him hear. . . . But the one who received the seed that fell on good soil is the man who hears the word and understands it. He produces a crop, yielding a hundred, sixty or thirty times what was sown."*

MATTHEW 13:3-4, 8-9, 23

---

In the Parable of the Sower, Jesus tells of a farmer tossing seed on four types of soil—the hard path, rocky ground, thorny ground, and good soil. Of course, we see four kinds of yields, too. Only the good soil produces what any harvester wants—a good crop. But Jesus wasn't really talking about soil; He was interested in hearts. In this parable He teaches that only a good heart produces good fruit.

In Ruth we see heart-soil like soft rich earth, so tillable. Her life obviously was not easy. Yet her flexible heart let God come in and work its soil. Her later fruitfulness was based on this work He did in her heart. So how do you respond to setbacks, hardships, and even tragedies in your life? Like Ruth, you can let them purify you and make your heart more flexible. If you want good heart-soil, you must let God come and break up its hardness, cast out its rocks, and uproot the thorns and briars. Then it will be prepared for a harvest of righteousness.

A flexible heart is fertile soil for the Gospel. Ruth's flexibility enabled her to marry into a Hebrew family and commit her life to their God, their values and customs. It enabled her to look beyond personal tragedy to fix her eyes in hope toward Israel. She did this even while witnessing Naomi's bitter disillusionment with God.

How difficult it is to continue in the company of a bitter person. Yet Ruth's character shone through her pain. Her heart never stiffened or hardened. If it had, she never could have received the abundant treasures of God's grace. We never hear Ruth snapping at Naomi or wallowing in self-pity over the loss of her own husband. Instead, she honors him by showing loyalty to his mother, his people, his country, and his God. She chooses to follow her mother-in-law not in weakness but with courage and dignity. Is there a person or circumstance that you can barely tolerate? Remember Ruth.

Neither is Ruth incapacitated by her poverty. Once in Israel, her flexible heart allows her to rise in self-sacrificing commitment rather than fall into self-absorbed resentment. Instead of feeling that the world owed her a living, she took the initiative and went to work, accepting a position lower than that of servants. She even drove the bitterness out of Naomi, giving her something to praise God for. Are there ways you need to follow her example?

Gleaning fields may have been a step below migrant farm work and a step above begging, something far beneath a woman of Ruth's quality. Many of us might fail to see God's providential care in an open door to glean fields. How many of us would be too proud, too narrow, too rigid to see God in such provision? We would much prefer to cast our eyes in another direction. Often with demanding spirits we expect God simply to dump the blessing on us. And we whine and become disillusioned when He does not. Far from embracing hardship, we long for the good life, for the life of ease, of comfort.

God was actively working behind the scenes in the drama of Ruth and Naomi to provide blessings much deeper than those on the surface. He was teaching them both lessons in faith, hope, character, and humility. Reduced to gleaning fields, Ruth accepted it gratefully.

Have you ever felt passed over and not used to your potential by

God or the church? So many of God's people feel called to a ministry because of their gift to preach, teach, sing, or play a musical instrument. They may work hard and earn all the right credentials; they may have all the energy, drive, and confidence in the world, and yet God "puts them on a shelf." They become disillusioned, wondering why God refuses to use them. What they do not realize, however, is that He cannot use them because they are still too enamored with themselves and driven by self-interest. With hearts that aren't flexible, they cannot bend down to the lowly task of becoming a simple servant. Having "despised the day of small things" (Zechariah 4:10), they are not prepared for great things.

---

*When he noticed how the guests picked the places of honor at the table, he told them this parable: "When someone invites you to a wedding feast, do not take the place of honor. . . . But when you are invited, take the lowest place, so that when your host comes, he will say to you, 'Friend, move up to a better place.' Then you will be honored in the presence of all your fellow guests. For everyone who exalts himself will be humbled, and he who humbles himself will be exalted."*

LUKE 14:7-8, 10-11

---

Henry Blackaby's book *Experiencing God* speaks of the need for adjusting one's life to God. He speaks of the many who want God to give them some special assignment but who are unwilling to make the major adjustments required. God cannot use them until they adjust to His purposes.

We would do well to examine our willingness to adjust to God and His will even when it requires costly sacrifice. To follow God and remain true to her commitments, Ruth made the proper adjustments. She always seemed to ask herself, "How can I make the best of this situation?"

Are you waiting for God to send you a blessing? Are you waiting for Him to show you a ministry? Are you waiting for Him to honor you? Then are you willing to follow His lead even when you don't like the path He assigns you? Be faithful to do whatever God sets before you. Jesus meant it when He told His followers the greatest would be the servant of all. The lowly task at hand may be exactly what God wants you to do. It will shape your character and may even be, as with Ruth, the vehicle to God's highest privileges.

You can choose your response to your circumstances. Ruth counted her blessings rather than her woes; her heart never hardened. Because Ruth's flexible heart allowed her to keep adjusting to drastic changes in her life, she could maintain godly character in every context. While her choices were intensely personal, everyone seemed to witness them. The Scripture says, "In the same way, good deeds are obvious, and even those that are not cannot be hidden" (1 Timothy 5:25). While Ruth had significant strikes against her—she was a widow, childless, poor, an outsider in a close-knit community—she managed to earn a sterling reputation. The entire community saw in her a virtuous woman who loved, worked hard, was faithful to God and family, and did everything with grace and dignity.

Your reputation, too, is formed as people watch you live out what you profess to believe. How loyal are you to God, your family and friends, and your church? Do others see a faithful, virtuous woman in you? Do you strive to do what is "right not only in the Lord's sight but also in the sight of others"?[3]

Ruth's sweaty labor tested her character, and that test of character opened new doors to her. The good reputation she won made Boaz sit up and take notice. She did not dream that when she refused to eat the bread of idleness, choosing to labor in a field under the hot sun day after day, she would become the beloved wife of that field's owner.

You may not be aware of God's sovereignty in your life, but as you go about your daily tasks, be open and flexible to His leading. Make the most of your hardships. Patiently allow God to forge His character in you through your trials and disappointments. Praise Him; trust Him. Be grateful to Him. He is working in ways you cannot see. For "we know that in all things God works for the good of those who love him, who have been called according to his purpose" (Romans 8:28).

Because Ruth kept her heart flexible, God guided her every step. She may not always have been aware of His leading, but she stayed open to new opportunities to grow and serve. Little did she know that her menial labor would one day make her, a seeming nobody, a direct ancestor to the Savior of the world. Likewise, God who sees our faithfulness, too, carefully weaves the circumstances of our lives together to honor and bless us, to fulfill His purpose for our lives.

Do you feel insignificant? Perhaps you have loved, served, followed, obeyed, and prayed, but you never married a rich Boaz or gained the approval of neighbors or even a mother-in-law. Carry on, hope on, trust on. Keep your heart soft and flexible toward God. You can count on it that somewhere, either in this life or in the next, your efforts will reap blessings of the highest magnitude. Your life and the seemingly insignificant decisions you make each day are eternally significant.

You may not yet see the larger purposes God has for your life, and you may never live up to the dreams you have for yourself or to the expectations that others have put on you. You may never see even a small fraction of the full worth of your contribution until the day when you look back through heaven's porthole and see your former struggles with clarity. You will then understand the significance your life held.

When you feel insignificant, remember Ruth the Moabitess and how a flexible heart succeeded in influencing not just a mother-in-law, a husband-to-be, and a community, but all of history. She was completely unaware of the eternal blessings God would bring to the world through her life.

If you, like Ruth, practice keeping your heart flexible to God's will, committing yourself to His sovereign purpose, He will pour into your life wondrous kingdom treasure. You, too, will reap the rewards of living a faithful life. Not only that, but you will influence history and by the lives you touch make your mark in eternity. Choose to trust God and allow Him to weave all your life's circumstances into something beautiful. Whatever the sacrifice, it is worth it.

## Heart Check

1. As you examine your heart, do you see it as flexible?

2. Think of a time when God asked you to do something difficult. Did you make the adjustment? If not, do you think you need to revisit this problem?

3. What steps can you take to have a more flexible heart like Ruth's?

4. What is the most important principle you can apply to your life from Ruth's example?

5. Compose a prayer to God in response to this chapter's lessons.

# 6

## THE HARDENED HEART

1 SAMUEL 14:49; 18–19; 25:44; 2 SAMUEL 3:13-16; 6:16-23;
1 CHRONICLES 15:27-29

THE YOUNG PRINCESS FELT HER heart skip a beat whenever she heard the courageous young warrior's name. King Saul's youngest daughter Michal would ultimately see her dreams come true. She would marry the heroic heartthrob, David. It was the stuff fairy tales are made of.

But this young woman whose heart had loved a man so fervently later came to despise this same man. With a heart callous, stony, and filled with evil treasure, she scathingly rebuked him for his uninhibited love for God. In Ruth we saw a flexible heart that enabled her to receive good treasure from God. She adjusted to her circumstances and stayed true to God and her loved ones. Not so with Michal. Her hard heart put a tragic ending to her love story. Therefore, we call her heart The Hardened Heart.

---

*Today, if you hear his voice, do not harden your hearts. . . . Let us, therefore, make every effort to enter that rest, so that no one will fall by following their example of disobedience.*

HEBREWS 4:7, 11

---

The story begins with David, the shepherd boy, going down to the battlefront where Israel and the Philistine army had faced off. The

Philistines had invaded Judah's territory, and King Saul had pledged his daughter in marriage to the man who would kill the Philistine champion Goliath. But all of Israel's mighty warriors—the entire army—had shrunk back in fear at the gigantic challenger's taunts.

David, however, the youngest of eight brothers and still only an adolescent, had bravely stepped forward with nothing more than "the name of the Lord," a slingshot, and a few stones. Single-handedly and without wearing armor, he killed Goliath and sent the entire Philistine army fleeing away. Instantly he became a hero in Israel and Judah; he was the talk of the entire kingdom. People came from all over the country to greet the returning victors, dancing for joy and singing, "Saul has slain his thousands, and David his tens of thousands" (1 Samuel 18:6-7). From that time on, everything David did was successful. He won every military campaign on which Saul sent him. All Israel and Judah adored him—especially Michal.

Saul owed his eldest daughter Merab's hand in marriage to David, but he reneged on his agreement. He was jealous and feared David, sensing in his spirit that David was his rival.

When Saul thought it might work to his own advantage, he finally offered Merab's hand in marriage to David if he would keep fighting Israel's battles. He figured the Philistines would soon kill David in a battle. But David refused to marry Merab, saying he felt unworthy to marry a king's daughter. So Saul gave Merab to another, and Michal, no doubt, could not have been happier.

Containing her love for David was hard for Michal. He was handsome and famous. His military exploits had become legendary. Yet he was not coarse like other warriors. He loved God deeply, something she could not really relate to but respected in him. He seemed so sensitive, a gifted harpist, composing and playing the sweetest, most inspiring music she had ever heard.

Michal's love for David became obvious to others, and when Saul heard about it, he was pleased—not for his daughter's sake, however. Again Saul sought to use a daughter to get rid of David. "I will give her to him," he thought, "so that she may be a snare to him" (1 Samuel 18:21).

When David again claimed his unworthiness, Saul laid a trap, making what he thought to be an impossible demand on David. Saul told him he could earn the right to marry Michal by killing 100 Philistines in a battle and bringing him their foreskins. David agreed and brought back twice as many. Therefore, Saul had to give Michal to David in marriage, both losing his daughter and making David, as his son-in-law, even more powerful.

Despite Saul's ill will, Michal began her life with David deeply satisfied. How could her father have done better in choosing a mate for her? How could God have blessed her more in granting her heart's desire? She could ask for nothing more.

For Saul, however, this was a distressing time. Seeing David's popularity, his success, and even Saul's own family members' affection for him drove Saul to distraction. Several times, afflicted by an evil spirit, he tried to kill David. Once he hurled a spear at the young man in his court as David played music on his harp for him. When David fled to his own home, Saul sent men to bring him back, intending to kill him. But Michal learned of the plan. "If you don't run for your life tonight," she warned her husband, "tomorrow you'll be killed" (1 Samuel 19:11). Knowing her father's spies were watching their door, she let him down through a window, and he escaped.

Meanwhile she fetched a life-sized idol—we might wonder why she had one—and put it in David's bed to make it look like he was asleep in it. When the men came for David, she said, "He is ill," and gave them a peek inside. They left and reported it to the king.

Saul, not at all pacified, sent them back again, telling them to bring David back with the bed, if they must. But David was gone, and when Saul found out, he summoned Michal. "Why did you deceive me like this and send my enemy away so that he escaped?" he demanded. Saving face and maybe her life, she replied, "He said to me, 'Let me get away. Why should I kill you?'" (1 Samuel 19:17). While daring to defy her maniac father to save David took real courage, Michal had accused her husband in a terrible way to save herself.

This episode earned Michal her father's anger, separation from her husband, and a mark on her own character. From then on, David

was a fugitive who could do nothing for his wife. One can only wonder whether she looked to the Lord or to her idol for solace. We don't
know anything about her faith. We do know she was a virtual hostage
whom Saul eventually punished by handing her over to another
man. Unlike her brother Jonathan, who had deep faith in God,
Michal apparently lacked a close relationship with God to carry her
through her tough times—and things got tougher. Ultimately the
Philistines killed Saul and three of Michal's brothers, including
Jonathan, in a battle. Somewhere in all this, her heart began to grow
hard and bitter.

After Saul's death, David was anointed Judah's king and reigned
in Hebron while Ishbosheth, Saul's surviving son, reigned as the king
of Israel. A struggle that "lasted a long time" ensued between the two
camps. David had reigned in Hebron for more than seven years when
Abner, the commander of Israel's army, decided to switch sides and
join David.

David told him, "I will make an agreement with you. But I
demand one thing of you: Do not come into my presence unless you
bring Michal daughter of Saul when you come to see me" (2 Samuel
3:13). Then David sent messengers to Ishbosheth, demanding
Michal's return.

By now it had been many years since David had seen Michal. He
had already collected several other wives. Thus he probably did not
demand Michal for reasons of love. More likely he thought his marriage to Saul's daughter would strengthen his claim to rule all of
Israel. Showing that he had no animosity toward Saul's house would
reunite the nation under him.

Ishbosheth, fearing David, took Michal from her second husband Paltiel. Poor Paltiel went weeping behind Michal for many
miles before Abner ordered him to go home. He could do nothing
but comply.

Still, this was not entirely a losing proposition for Michal. Her
return to David would restore her from relative insignificance to
prominence. As Saul's daughter and David's first wife, hers would be
an important position in the kingdom above the other wives.

In time, after Ishbosheth's own men murdered him, all Israel came to David's side to make him their king. With his power consolidated and every enemy defeated, all the world respected King David: "So David's fame spread throughout every land, and the LORD made all the nations fear him" (1 Chronicles 14:17).

While David transformed Jerusalem into the nation's capital and his royal city, he also wanted to make it the national center of worship. To do so, he earnestly desired to bring the Ark of God there. We must know the Ark's significance in order to understand his intensity in this matter.

The Ark was the national symbol of God's covenant with Israel, a national treasure, Israel's most sacred object. It was constructed according to God's precise dictate and contained the stone tablets upon which He had inscribed the Ten Commandments. The high priest entered the Holy of Holies once a year to sprinkle blood over the Ark's "mercy seat" to atone for the sins of the entire nation. The waters of the Jordan River had parted before the Ark as the nation followed it into the Promised Land. It went before Israel in battle, symbolizing God's presence with His people. It was said that the Lord Almighty was enthroned between the cherubim on the Ark's mercy seat.

Yet a period of serious decline and corruption came to Israel under the rule of the judges. Priest and judge Eli died along with his two corrupt sons. The Philistines defeated Israel in a war and captured the Ark. Evidently they destroyed Shiloh, a center of worship where the Ark had been kept. Thus when the Philistines returned the Ark to Israel because of the curses it brought upon them, Israel had no place for it. For twenty years a man named Abinadab kept the Ark in his house. Saul became Israel's first king but had little heart for God or for the Ark. We find it briefly mentioned once during his reign.

Then came King David—the man after God's own heart. David wanted God's blessing on Israel under his kingship. As the new king, he conquered Jerusalem and set it up as his capital city—the City of David. From the beginning, he wanted to build a temple to glorify the

Lord, reunite the nation's worship, and help abolish idolatrous influences. His dream began with retrieving the Ark and bringing it to Jerusalem. More than a national treasure to David, it was a treasure he held in his heart because he loved God.

His first attempt to bring the Ark to Jerusalem shook David to his core when God struck Uzzah dead for unlawfully grasping it. David made sure his next attempt would be done in the prescribed way. He set to work making all the right preparations. He made the priests consecrate themselves. Then he appointed the Levitical leaders to assemble choirs of singers to sing joyful songs with various musical instruments accompanying them. He appointed some to be doorkeepers of the Ark, to walk before it and sound trumpets. These, along with all of Israel's elders and the commanders of units of a thousand, would go with David to bring up the Ark from the house of Obed-Edom to Jerusalem.

David wrote a psalm of praise for the occasion, committing it to Asaph and his associates to sing:

---

*O give thanks to the LORD, call on his name, make known his deeds among the peoples. Sing to him, sing praises to him, tell of all his wonderful works. Glory in his holy name; let the hearts of those who seek the LORD rejoice. . . . Sing to the LORD, all the earth. Tell of his salvation from day to day. Declare his glory among the nations, his marvelous works among all the peoples. For great is the LORD, and greatly to be praised; he is to be revered above all gods. For all the gods of the peoples are idols, but the LORD made the heavens. Honor and majesty are before him; strength and joy are in his place. Ascribe to the LORD, O families of the peoples, ascribe to the LORD glory and strength. Ascribe to the LORD the glory due his name; bring an offering, and come before him. Worship the LORD in holy splendor.*

1 CHRONICLES 16:8-10, 23-29

---

On the big day David could hardly contain his joy. All Israel assembled along the parade route to see the Ark brought up to the place David had prepared for it. Imagine the scene. As the joyful procession neared Jerusalem, this time with God's approval, the celebration became louder and louder. Trumpets blaring, cymbals crashing, and throngs of people roaring exuberantly—the sound must have been deafening. David had never felt such ecstatic joy. Wearing a linen ephod, a sleeveless garment that all the Levites and singers also wore, he broke out in wholehearted and exuberant dancing before the Lord.

Now Michal had a good view from her palace window aloft the parade route. Staring impassively at the commotion below, she suddenly did a double take. Could her eyes be deceiving her? She saw the female dancers festively performing, and that was acceptable. But who was that man leaping and prancing and cavorting like a fool? She stared hard. What? It—it was her husband—DAVID! He had shed his royal robes and was wearing a mere linen garment. How—how could he?

Michal was dumbfounded. *He's the king!* she thought. *Where's his sense of propriety, of dignity, of decorum?* Michal had far more concern for the king's reputation than for the arrival of the Ark. What she could not understand was that David did not want to appear as the proud king but as the humble servant. The almighty and holy God had raised him up from a lowly shepherd boy to the pinnacle of kingly power. David felt it entirely fitting to cast aside his royal robe and dress as the priests and Levites to appear with them as a servant of God. He felt it completely appropriate to rollick with the "commoners" from among whom he had risen. So while David danced, Michal glowered sullenly, possibly wearing the only scowl in all of Israel that day.

David had won many victories, but this was the happiest day of his life. While he laughed and sang joyfully in the streets like a child, Michal, not at all understanding his heart, thought, *What a disgusting spectacle!* The Bible says, "And when she saw King David leaping and dancing before the Lord, she despised him in her heart." Somewhere life had hardened Michal. The doting, young princess, full of love and passion, had become a cold, hardhearted queen. While she had once loved David and even risked her life for him, she now abhorred him. She did not share his passion for God. Her father Saul had cared little for the Ark; neither did she. This great day for the kingdom and for David meant nothing to her. David's joyful exuberance only hardened her the more, filling her with angry disdain. Her heart had become filled with evil treasure.

After the Ark was set in the temporary tent David had pitched for it, they sacrificed all their burnt offerings and fellowship offerings to the Lord. Then David blessed all the people and sent them home with generous gifts of bread, dates, and raisins.

David could hardly wait to get back to his own home to share his joy and blessings with his own household. It had been an awesome day, the fulfillment of his dreams, his restoration from all those years of being pursued by Saul like a criminal. Through it all he had managed to keep his integrity, trusting God to vindicate him, and God had proved faithful. David had never loved the Lord more.

Bursting into his palace with joy, he was ready to continue the celebration. But Michal would have none of it. Believing David had left his dignity out in the street, she had been waiting for him, ready to sober him with a tongue-lashing. "How the king of Israel has distinguished himself today, disrobing in the sight of the slave girls of his servants as any vulgar fellow would!"

Her acid words stung the king. He stared at her, mortified, no longer seeing his wife but seeing instead the daughter of the man who had earlier thrown spears at him. As Saul's daughter, she may have suddenly represented all the tormenting years that had continually hounded him, trying to deny him this day for which he was destined. He fired back, "It was before the LORD, who chose me rather than your father or anyone from his house when he appointed me ruler over the LORD's people Israel—I will celebrate before the LORD. I will become even more undignified than this, and I will be humiliated in my own eyes. But by these slave girls you spoke of, I will be held in honor" (2 Samuel 6:20-22).

There is more to this story than meets the eye. This was an incredibly significant time in the nation's history—possibly like America's Bicentennial. If all Israel rejoiced with David so exuberantly, where was Michal? She was not found along the parade route frolicking beside her husband and king. Instead she was up in a window coldly looking down, prepared to have her husband stand stoically beside her, nodding his head to the crowd benevolently and waving loftily. Disgusted and alone, she peered out and saw her husband acting like a commoner, and she despised him in her heart. A time in Israel's history to treasure could not move her. She had let her heart calcify, and the joy of that special moment could not penetrate it.

We don't know the reasons for Michal's hardness. Perhaps she simply viewed David's grand entrance into the city as undignified, believing that a king should show no emotion. Perhaps she had no use for public worship. Perhaps it began much earlier when David took her from Paltiel. For much of her life, Michal had been a pawn, the victim of political intrigue with little influence over her own life. Still, no one could own Michal's heart. She had power within to choose her destiny—and she did. She chose to sin against David, and she chose to be disloyal and unsupportive of God's work. Her hardened heart ruined her relationship with David that day. Whatever love he had for her died, and their marriage virtually ended. She lived on in the palace as queen, but we hear nothing more of her except these final sad words: "And Michal the daughter of Saul had no child to the day of her death."[1]

How different this story might have been if only Michal's heart had been as open to God's treasure as her husband's.

## LESSONS FOR OUR OWN HEARTS

Her unfruitful womb was tragedy enough for Michal. The greater tragedy, however, was her hardened heart that made her whole life unfruitful. A cold, unproductive heart cannot receive God's treasures and cannot bear any good fruit. In the last chapter we looked at Jesus' Parable of the Sower. Ruth's heart was the good, rich soil, but Michal's heart is best represented by the hard-baked ground of a well-worn footpath. Since seeds cannot penetrate this environment, birds come and eat them. In the parable Jesus points out that the truth of God's Word cannot penetrate a hardened heart.

---

*Plow up the hardness of your hearts; otherwise the good seed will be wasted among the thorns.*

JEREMIAH 4:3 TLB

---

We must allow God to break up the hardened soil of our hearts. While we do not bear full responsibility for what befalls us in life, we are responsible for how we choose to respond. Let's look at some issues we must deal with if we want God to make us fruitful for His glory.

## The Issue of Surrender

I had not yet surrendered my life to Christ for salvation; however, He was knocking hard on my heart's door. "Give me your heart," He said. But I looked down at my heart and saw nothing but hardness. I felt this old petrified thing in my chest with its door rusted shut and replied, "I don't feel as if I have a heart left." It was true—life had seriously damaged my heart, but He said, "You do. Give it to Me." All I had to do was turn it over to Him so He could do the work. When I finally surrendered my heart to Him, His love melted my hardness, and He began His healing work.

---

*I will give you a new heart and put a new spirit in you; I will remove from you your heart of stone and give you a heart of flesh.*

EZEKIEL 36:26

---

How often since that initial transaction have I still pulled away, not wanting Him to take parts of my hardness; I hold on to the stubborn places, insisting on my own way. Years have come and gone, and He still must work on my heart. At times, when I get angry from being wounded, weary, or discouraged, my heart begins to harden

again, and a spiritual rigor mortis sets in. Finally I desperately cry out
to God as in the words of Keith Green:

> *Oh what can be done with an old heart like mine?*
> *Soften it up with Your oil and wine.*

The song went on to explain that the oil represents God's Holy
Spirit and the wine His blood. Turning that old heart of mine over to
Him, He starts softening it up again, renewing it with the treasures
of His life.

Continual stubbornness hardens us. This was the case with
the children of Israel. After God delivered them from Egypt, dis-
contentment, defiance, disobedience, and defeat marked their
sojourn. "Do not harden your hearts," God warns, "as you did at
Meribah, as you did that day at Massah in the desert" (Psalm 95:8).
Michal's refusal to surrender to God's purpose on that joyous day
in Israel did not result from one sudden isolated decision but from
a series of choices that culminated in hatred. As we resist God's
will, our hearts surely harden, and we cut off the treasure of His
grace.

To prevent our hearts from hardening, we must stay surrendered to Jesus Christ. Such victory will require drawing near to
Him, spending time with Him, abiding in Him, receiving His
"oil and wine." Then, and only then, can we experience the love
of God melting the hardness of our stubborn hearts. This is the
only way to make it in this heart-hardening, soul-destroying
world.

In the parable of the wineskins, Jesus said He must pour His
new wine into new wineskins. Why? Because old ones have become
too hard and brittle to hold new wine. They will burst and ruin the
wine.[2] Our hearts can become like those old wineskins—hard and
rigid, unable to accept Christ's lordship and therefore unable to
receive His spiritual treasure. By surrendering our hearts, we will be
pliable and open to the "new" things God wants to do in, through,
and around us.

## The Issue of Love and Forgiveness

How quickly and easily we can become embittered when life unexpectedly twists us in painful directions. Both Ruth and Michal had bad experiences—both lost family members, including their husbands; both lived through major upheavals. Yet Ruth's bitter experiences did not make her bitter. She was willing to follow God, while Michal was not.

In one way Michal was a victim. She had some big disappointments in her life. Not only had she suffered the loss of family members, but also she had suffered the effects of growing up in a dysfunctional home. As a princess, she saw her father crazily fly into fits of rage and even throw spears at people. Used as a pawn for political reasons, Saul gave her first to David and then to another man. She had loved David, lost him, been loved by another man, lost him, and now she had David again and just didn't know what she thought anymore. Yes, she was a victim.

Yet in another way, Michal victimized herself. She held onto her grudges, not forgiving, not allowing her heart to melt in God's love and grace. Whatever caused Michal's bitterness toward David, she needed to forgive him, and she needed to forgive God. If only she had let go of her bitterness, she could have joined her husband, rejoicing with him in his happiest moment. He would have loved her; their hearts would have knit together. But instead, pulling back and watching scornfully from her window perch, she killed love that day. She didn't know that when she let bitterness cause her to despise her husband, she was also disdaining God and sealing her destiny.

---

*But by your hard and impenitent heart you are storing up wrath for yourself on the day of wrath, when God's righteous judgment will be revealed.*

ROMANS 2:5 NRSV

---

We shut ourselves out from the treasures of God's grace when we refuse to let His love penetrate our hearts. All of us have experienced wounds, disappointments, and disillusionments. Entertaining a root of bitterness solves nothing for us. It neither removes nor changes the bad circumstances. It only worsens our situation and hands us a life of defeat. If we respond to God, on the other hand, offering our hearts to him, we give Him an opportunity to bring good from our situation.

An elderly woman I once worked for, named Verna, had a disease that kept her in a wheelchair. She was a bitter person. One day I pried a bit to find out the root of her bitterness. When she was sixteen, she had applied to a large church for funds so she could go to a music academy. The church turned her down, and she had never forgiven them. The incident was as fresh in her mind as it had been over fifty years before. I tried to minister to her, but she had completely hardened her heart, refusing to give it back to God. I suspected that her illness was even related to the bitter treasure that she had let poison her heart. Sometime later she was burned to death when she dropped a cigarette in her lap. What a tragic life; what a tragic end.

Have you hardened your heart in your distress? Do you resent certain people? Are there those with whom you will not speak, whom you have not forgiven? Bitterness will always rupture your relationship with God and result in a fruitless, barren life.

We should be like David. When sitting in a cave hiding from Saul, he had every human reason to be bitter. Refusing to entertain that bitterness, however, he cried out to God: "Be merciful to me, O God, be merciful to me, for in you my soul takes refuge; in the shadow of your wings I will take refuge, until the destroying storms pass by. I cry to God Most High, to God who fulfills his purpose for me" (Psalm 57:1-2 NRSV).

### The Issue of Worship

Think of the historic event in which Michal might have participated; think of the joy she could have shared, not only with her husband but with all of Israel. Yet she could not worship. Keeping a safe distance from the revelers in the street, she was too proud and aloof for such "carryings on."

---

*As it is said, "Today, if you hear his voice, do not harden your hearts as in the rebellion."*

HEBREWS 3:15 NRSV

---

Michal's sarcasm toward David exposed the hardness of heart that resulted in her rejecting not only David but also God. Nothing suggests that David was dressed indecently at this celebration. Michal, however, thought that David had violated his kingly dignity by shedding his regal robes and lowering himself to the level of a priest. In her mind he had made a fool of himself before slave girls. She was more concerned with his maintaining the dignity of his position than with rejoicing before God for the arrival of the Ark of the Covenant.

The frightening thing about Michal's condition is that she felt she was so "right." The self-righteous sins are difficult to detect in ourselves. We have a principle. David violated Michal's principle—what she considered behavior befitting a king. He had disgraced himself and embarrassed her, and she felt wholly justified in her rebuke. But beneath this principle may be something even more ugly in Michal's soul: Because she could not love God, she hated her husband for loving Him.

The church has experienced "worship wars" in recent decades. We get so hung up on styles of worship, but that is not the real issue. The issue is loving God and expressing that love for Him. All styles of worship can glorify the Lord, but sometimes God wants to do something new. He sees us bored and complacent, locked into our traditions or rituals, loving them more than we love Him. With hearts dead, unfeeling, and unresponsive toward Him, we feel nothing of the joy and gratefulness that befits our salvation. Thus any exuberance seems unfitting. We see one like David—alive and uninhibited with love for God—and our sense of dignity is offended. But is it really "dignity" to heap scorn on the wholehearted worship and celebration of our Lord and King?

The fact is, if we do not worship, our hearts will become hard.

While we should avoid creating "norms" or stereotypes of appropriate worship, a heart filled with good treasure is a worshiping heart. As we yield our hearts to the Spirit of God, He will enable us to worship ever more freely—without fears, inhibitions, or excessive concern for the expectations of others. If we worship—even giving a "sacrifice of praise" when we do not feel like it—our hearts will soften. Whatever we have been through, worship has the power to melt away the pain and hardness in our hearts.

We should always remember: Worship is for an audience of One. It is not about "my" preferences or "my" desires; it is about *God* and His worthiness to be worshiped. If we allow ourselves to get bitter over worship styles and preferences, judging others as Michal did, we will lose a great deal of the treasure God wants to deposit in our hearts.

---

*Sow for yourselves righteousness; reap steadfast love; break up your fallow ground; for it is time to seek the LORD, that he may come and rain righteousness upon you.*

HOSEA 10:12 NRSV

---

What kind of heart-hardening sin is in your life? Plow up your fallow ground the way a plow breaks up ground. Ask God to replace any stoniness in your heart so He can make it soft and pliable, trusting and open to change.

Michal had the royal pedigree; she was the daughter of Israel's first king and the wife of Israel's second. By all rights, she could and should have been in Christ's lineage. But having disqualified herself with her hard, deaf heart of stone, God passed her by. She was barren and fruitless to the day of her death.

Ruth's name, on the other hand, had never graced any registry of nobility. She had no credentials at all. But her heart allowed her to be fruitful. She gained the privilege of having her name added to the genealogy of Jesus Christ, the world's Messiah. Clearly, the treasure of one's heart means far more to God than worldly credentials.

If Michal had taken note of her heart's condition and cried out to God for mercy, she could have become all God intended for her to be. He would have filled her heart with the riches of His kingdom treasure. If only she had cried out with David, "Create in me a clean heart, O God, and put a new and right spirit within me. Do not cast me away from your presence, and do not take your Holy Spirit from me. Restore to me the joy of your salvation, and sustain in me a willing spirit" (Psalm 51:10-12 NRSV).

### *Heart Check*

1. As you see the opposite outcomes of these two women's lives, which kind of heart would you have represent your own?

2. Think about the issues of surrender, love and forgiveness, and worship. Are you pleasing God in these areas?

3. Are there places of stoniness in your heart that hinder your relationship with God? What steps can you take to make your heart more tender, receptive, and responsive to God's will and purpose?

4. What is the most important principle you can apply to your life from Michal's example?

5. Compose a prayer to God in response to this chapter's lessons.

# 7

## *Sarah (Sarai)*

### THE FAITHFUL HEART

GENESIS 11–25; ISAIAH 51:2; ROMANS 4:19; 9:9;
HEBREWS 11:11; 1 PETER 3:6

HER NAME MEANS PRINCESS, queen, or chieftainness. Sarah's stunning beauty befitted her name. The book of Genesis devotes more space to her and Abraham's story than to the entire human race preceding them. As the wife of the first Hebrew and the mother of the nation of Israel, she ranks as one of the most important women in world history.

---

*Listen to me, you who pursue righteousness and who seek the LORD: Look to the rock from which you were cut and to the quarry from which you were hewn; look to Abraham, your father, and to Sarah, who gave you birth.*

ISAIAH 51:1-2

---

At first called Sarai, she received her new name from God late in life as a sign and seal of His covenantal promise given to her husband to make her the mother of nations: "I will bless her so that she will be the mother of nations; kings of peoples will come from her" (Genesis 17:16). Besides Israel, other nations and kings would be descended from her. In her grandson Esau's genealogy, we read of her descendants, "These were the kings who reigned in Edom. . . ."[1] Most important, however, she was the progenitor of Jesus Christ, the King of kings and Lord of lords. In Him we see the spiritual fulfillment of God's promise. His spiritual seed would birth multitudes of believers from every nation—making them "kings and priests unto God."[2]

But the fulfillment of God's glorious promise would not come easily for Sarah. It would be a bumpy ride on the road to becoming the mother of nations. She first had to endure a long life of testing through which she learned the difficult lessons of faith, patience, and sacrifice.

Sarah was a woman of strong personality. But she faithfully obeyed both God and her husband Abram (later called Abraham). Her love for Abram nearly knew no bounds. If Abram would leave his home and country to follow God's call on his life, she would leave to follow Abram. Forsaking her way of life, she went wherever he went. His life became her life. She did her best to adjust to the many sacrifices required of her. Through ups and downs, joys and sorrows, triumphs and failures, she refused to look back.

It is said of Abraham that God "found his heart faithful."[3] Because Sarah was so closely aligned with her husband, we will call her heart The Faithful Heart. Sometimes Abraham made foolish decisions that drastically affected her life. In her heart, however, she would always "stand by her man." Yes, she had her failings, too. But she never turned from what she believed was God's intent. She had good treasure in her heart that kept her true to her calling. For the better part of a century, she faithfully lived as a nomad and stranger, going in and out of foreign lands. Together she and Abraham experienced dangers, hardships, and disappointments as they searched for "a country of their own."[4]

We first see Sarah in Scripture in her father-in-law Terah's genealogy: "The name of Abram's wife was Sarai. . . . Now Sarai was barren; she had no children." She no doubt lived with intense feelings of guilt and failure, because a woman was of little importance until she could bear a son to carry on her husband's legacy.

Yet God had grand plans for Sarai and Abram. Through this chosen couple, He planned to create a chosen people—a God-centered, moral nation that He could bless and call His own, that would in turn influence and bless the entire world. One day God said to Abram,

"Leave your country, your people and your father's household and go to the land I will show you. I will make you into a great nation and I will bless you. . . . and all peoples on earth will be blessed through you" (Genesis 12:1-3).

Abram was seventy-five and Sarai about sixty-five years of age, and they were well settled in their affluent community when God asked them to leave for a destination unknown. Land, family, and inheritance were significant in ancient society. His father's household identified a man. When the head of a household died, his heir assumed his headship, along with ancestral lands and property. In leaving his father's household, Abram forfeited his inheritance. Some ancient Near Eastern cultures even believed that neglecting aged parents and not giving them proper burials meant forfeiting a pleasant afterlife.

Yet Abram obeyed God, and Sarai aligned herself with his decision. We never see in Abram a man who commanded, "Now submit, woman!" And we never see in Sarai a woman who said, "I will not!" They set out with one heart, putting their identity, security, destiny, and very lives into the Lord's hands. They did have personal wealth—including possessions, servants, flocks, and herds—which they took with them. Their nephew Lot also came along.

When their caravan reached Shechem in Canaan, the Lord appeared to Abram and promised, "To your offspring I will give this land" (Genesis 12:7). So Abram built an altar in the Lord's honor, and Sarai probably worshiped there with him. For she, too, trusted the God who had called her husband. Together they were becoming "heirs of the gracious gift of life."[5]

From there they went to the hills near Bethel where Abram built a second altar and called on the Lord. Then seeking relief from a severe famine, they journeyed into Egypt. We never see Sarai deriding Abram, complaining, "I told you so; we should never have left home." No, trouble could not shake her loyalty, nor could Abram's ill-conceived ideas—and it was good for Abram that this was so!

Sarai may have been one of the most beautiful women ever to live. Although she was now between sixty-five and seventy years of age, she still was attractive. Having seen admiring eyes cast on his wife everywhere they went, Abram lived in fear. The thought of entering territories where godless monarchs cruelly resorted to any means to get what they wanted terrified him. He felt sure they would see his wife, kill him, and seize her for themselves.

In Egypt this fear became uppermost in his mind, and he devised a scheme—a cowardly one at best. Because Sarai and he both had the same father, Terah, but different mothers, Sarai was his half-sister. Such marriages were common in this early patriarchal era, and he decided to use it to his advantage. He would say he was her brother. As brother, he would be honored; as husband, however, he might be killed.

Therefore, as they were about to enter Egypt, he turned to Sarai and said, "Say you are my sister, so that I will be treated well for your sake and my life will be spared because of you." If she at all wondered, "Doesn't Abram love me?" it was buried by her greater question, "How can I help spare Abram's life?" She went along with the scheme; besides, it was a half-truth and not a full lie.

The Egyptians did indeed notice Sarai. Pharaoh's officials believed Abram's word that she was his sister. So they went immediately and "praised her to Pharaoh."[6] The Hebrew word for their commendation—*halal*—is used here in the Bible for the first time. In that this word is nearly always used for praising God, it seems to suggest a special significance here. Impressed with more than her exquisite physical beauty, the men must also have seen Sarai as a uniquely praiseworthy woman—a "princess" as her name suggests—in bearing and character. Their report so impressed Pharaoh that he sent for her and took her into his courts. Rather than degrading her, however, he considered her for marriage.

For the favor Pharaoh gave Abram a considerable dowry of herds, flocks, and camels, along with more men and maidservants. Still, we can imagine Sarai and Abram spending sleepless nights, trying to figure a way out of their disaster. Fortunately, having "the mother of nations" put in this position displeased God, who acted by sending plagues upon Pharaoh's entire household. Pharaoh summoned Abram and asked him, "What have you done to me? Why didn't you tell me she was your wife? Why did you say, 'She is my sister,' so that I took her to be my wife? Now then, here is your wife. Take her and go!" (Genesis 12:18-19).

Journeying back to Bethel, the two no doubt felt ashamed but glad to be alive. At Bethel Abram called on the Lord. Soon afterward Lot left to dwell near Sodom and Gomorrah in the Jordan plain. Then God reaffirmed his covenant with Abram, promising, "All the land that you see I will give to you and your offspring for ever. I will make your offspring like the dust of the earth" (Genesis 13:15-16).

God continued to prosper Abram and Sarai. They watched their wealth grow and multiply daily. When Lot got caught in a war and was carried off, Abram rescued him with some 318 trained menservants who had been born in his household. Those left to attend his property must have been a good number also. Sarai probably exercised authority over this vast household in his absence. Still, despite all their wealth, what she wanted most in life—a son—was denied her.

Abram, too, was anxious for an heir. He had trusted God's sovereignty, never complaining to Sarai or blaming her, but now her childbearing years were surely past, and what was he to think? God saw his drooping faith and came to him in a vision. "Do not be afraid, Abram," He said. "I am your shield, your very great reward." Less than encouraged, Abram lamented, "O Sovereign LORD, what can you give me since I remain childless. . . . You have given me no children; so a servant in my household will be my heir."

The Lord assured him, "A son coming from your own body will be your heir. Look up at the heavens and count the stars—if indeed you can count them. So shall your offspring be." Well, this was just what Abram had needed! Scripture says, "Abram believed the LORD, and he credited it to him as righteousness" (Genesis 15:1-6).

But what about Sarai? She had for too long borne the pain of failure. She had waited year in and year out, faithfully hanging onto God's promise. Finally she lost the capacity to have children. Looking down at her aging, sagging body, she thought, *The promise never included me; I had only hoped so. How foolish of me to have thought the promised son would be mine.* So her gnawing sense of failure over their empty cradle remained. She thought of the quiet grief her dear husband had borne for so many years. Now he had renewed hope. Still, did God really speak to him, or did he imagine it? Oh, whatever! How could she bear to see his hope dashed again?

Even faithful hearts can be deceived. Suddenly Sarai thought, *God must be waiting for me to do my part before He does His part.* Yes, she must help God along. As a last resort—at least in her mind—she thought of how to solve their problem. It must have been an extremely distasteful solution to her but the only one she could imagine. Resorting to human strategy to accomplish the divine purpose, she went to Abram and offered him her most trusted servant Hagar, saying, "The LORD has kept me from having children. Go, sleep with my maidservant; perhaps I can build a family through her" (Genesis 16:2).

Abram consented to Sarai's solution, probably thinking, *Well, why not? This must be it!* Why did this solution seem plausible to them? It was legal. Because failure to produce an heir meant major calamity for families in ancient societies, they developed legal remedies allowing a man whose wife had not borne him a son to impregnate a slave girl. The father could then consider the offspring as his heirs (Code of Hammurabi[7]). Hagar was, in effect, Sarai's own property; any child she bore would legally be Sarai's.

Abram slept with Hagar, and she quickly conceived, finally giving the eighty-six-year-old man hope for a son. But all was not perfect. Hagar knew Abram's hopes rested on her son. Now elevated from the status of a lowly servant to the mother of her master's son, she began to see Sarai as her rival. Thinking in her mind that she was the better woman, the most favored by God, and the most highly regarded by Abram, she haughtily disdained her mistress.

This became unbearable for Sarai. Convinced that Abram had given Hagar reason for her uppityness, she barked, "You are responsible for the wrong I am suffering. I put my servant in your arms, and now that she knows she is pregnant, she despises me. May the LORD judge between you and me."

If Abram had done anything to encourage Hagar's behavior, he immediately corrected it. "Your servant is in your hands," he said.

"Do with her whatever you think best" (Genesis 16:5-6). So Sarai acted quickly and punitively. Hagar fled into the wilderness where an angel told her to return and be submissive to Sarai.

This seemed to solve things for a long time, and Sarai doubtless treated Abram's son Ishmael as the child of promise. But their natural solution had not been God's will. The first heir of the redemptive covenant was not destined to come through natural means but by obvious divine intervention.

Evidently Abram did not hear from the Lord again for another thirteen years when suddenly He appeared. He changed Abram's name to Abraham, meaning "father of many," and reaffirmed His promise. Abraham had been certain Ishmael was the rightful heir. For the past thirteen years, he, Sarai, and Hagar, along with all the rest of his household, considered nothing else.

But God had a shock for Abraham: "As for Sarai your wife," He said, "you are no longer to call her Sarai; her name will be Sarah. I will bless her and will surely give you a son by her. I will bless her so that she will be the mother of nations; kings of peoples will come from her."

If we notice the "ha" added to Abraham's name change, it seems God Himself was anticipating Abraham's reaction. Indeed Abraham fell on his face laughing! Then he burst out, "Will a son be born to a man a hundred years old? Will Sarah bear a child at the age of ninety?" Content with Ishmael, he added, "If only Ishmael might live under your blessing!"

But God was adamant: "Yes, but your wife Sarah will bear you a son, and you will call him Isaac. I will establish my covenant with him as an everlasting covenant for his descendants after him." He promised that Ishmael, too, would father a great nation. "But my covenant I will establish with Isaac, whom Sarah will bear to you by this time next year" (Genesis 17:15-21).

Perhaps Abraham told his wife about this latest divine visitation, but postmenopausal Sarah must have passed it off, thinking he was suffering from the heat. One day, however, heavenly visitors came to confirm it. Since women did not sit at the table with men, especially not with strangers, Abraham entertained the three in his tent while Sarah stayed out of sight. Even so, the Lord made sure she was within hearing. Without doubt, her faith was weak, and since she must conceive by faith, they wanted her to hear the promise for herself. "Where is your wife, Sarah?" she heard them ask. In saying her name, they showed their familiarity with her and drew her to eavesdrop attentively.

Then one said, "I will surely return to you about this time next year, and Sarah your wife will have a son." Sarah could not believe her ears. How could she know the joy of motherhood now? Not only was she past childbearing years, but she had been barren even when young. No one had ever heard of such a thing, and it was simply too farfetched. So as Abraham had previously laughed, she now laughed too, thinking, *After I am worn out and my master is old, will I now have this pleasure?* She had laughed to herself, but the Lord asked, "Why did Sarah laugh and say, 'Will I really have a child, now that I am old?'" Oh-oh, Sarah was busted. She froze.

"Is anything too hard for the LORD?" He asked. In asking the question, He answered it. Of course, the God who made all physical laws could change them if He chose. Then He repeated His promise: "I will return to you at the appointed time next year and Sarah will have a son."

Frightened, Sarah called out, "I did not laugh." But He insisted, "Yes, you did laugh." He didn't reprimand her sharply but lovingly (Genesis 18:9-15). She knew in her heart that God had spoken. All these years she had faithfully believed in Him and followed His instructions through her husband, but now He had sent a word directly to her. He would bring life to her dead womb. What was laughable would truly happen.

After this Abraham led his caravan into the Negev. Even at ninety years old, Sarah was so sufficiently preserved that Abraham still feared that kings would fall for her. So again he told the half-lie; again he exposed Sarah to great peril; again he imperiled God's plan to make of them a great nation; again Sarah went along with it. Hadn't they learned anything the last time?

Sure enough, Abimelech, the Philistine king, admired Sarah and took her into his harem. Before the king could touch her, however, God intervened. Visiting the king in a dream, He threatened, "You are as good as dead because of the woman you have taken; she is a married woman." When Abimelech told his officials, they were all likewise terrified. He summoned Abraham, who explained that when they had first begun to sojourn in foreign lands, he had told Sarah, "This is how you can show your love to me: Everywhere we go, say of me, 'He is my brother'" (Genesis 20:3-13). What a sad abuse of a faithful wife. As they left there, Abraham likely promised Sarah that he had finally learned his lesson.

Despite this mishap, precisely at the time God had said, He made good on His promise. Sarah became pregnant, and the laughter of the annunciation became the joy of fulfillment. She could finally give her centenarian husband a son, for "the Lord was gracious to Sarah just as He said." Imagine what this child meant to her. Filled with joy and wonder, she would laugh as he nursed at her breast.

They named their son Isaac, meaning "laughter." Sarah exulted, "God has brought me laughter, and everyone who hears about this will laugh with me. Who would have said to Abraham that Sarah would nurse children? Yet I have borne him a son in his old age." Indeed Isaac's birth was humanly impossible; God had done a restorative miracle.

On the day Isaac was weaned—a significant rite of passage in ancient times—Abraham celebrated by holding a great public feast. Not only would there be a large number of servants present but also many people of the land who knew of the miraculous birth.

At the feast Sarah suddenly spotted Ishmael mocking Isaac for all the fuss over him. So many had laughed *with* Sarah at Isaac's birth, but Ishmael was laughing *at* him, probably reflecting his mother's attitude. Sarah had never trusted Hagar since their previous years of strife, and now she sensed dangerous rivalry ahead. She immediately called Abraham aside. "Get rid of that slave woman and her son," she demanded, "for that slave woman's son will never share in the inheritance with my son Isaac."

Sarah may have been harsh, but she clearly saw the issues at stake. Young Isaac did not need a resentful half-brother fourteen years his senior and the boy's jealous mother abusing him. But beyond this difficulty, the covenant promises made to Isaac were at risk. What if Abraham and Sarah died? How would Isaac defend himself against these two? Yet Sarah's attitude toward Ishmael alarmed Abraham. Thus God addressed him, saying, "Do not be so distressed about the boy and your maidservant. Listen to whatever Sarah tells you, because it is through Isaac that your offspring will be reckoned" (Genesis 21:1-12).

The apostle Paul says of the incident, "At that time the son born in the ordinary way persecuted the son born by the power of the Spirit" (Galatians 4:29). Viewing Sarah's words as prophetically inspired for all of God's children born of the Spirit, Paul refers to them: "But what does the Scripture say? 'Get rid of the slave woman and her son, for the slave woman's son will never share in the inheritance with the free woman's son.' Therefore, brothers, we are not children of the slave woman, but of the free woman" (Galatians 4:30-31).

Finally convinced that Sarah was right, that the two families could not simply coexist, Abraham sent Ishmael and Hagar away early the next morning. With Isaac's position now secure, Sarah could raise him as the child of promise without fear.

There is no record of Sarah in the years following this experience. We can assume she continued to stand faithfully by her husband and raise her son to love God. Then at the age of 127, Sarah's long and turbulent life of steadfast devotion came to its earthly end. She had sojourned by her husband's side in the land of Canaan for over sixty years. In that she is the only woman whose age at death the Bible records, we see how prominently she figured in the hearts of the early Hebrews.

Abraham had loved Sarah dearly, and it must have grieved him greatly to lose his beloved life partner. He went to her tent and mourned and wept over her body. Then wanting a more permanent resting place for her, he broke with the ancient custom of desert burial by purchasing a field with a cave for her burial. When he himself died, his sons buried him beside her. Isaac so loved his mother that only his marriage to Rebekah could bring him comfort after his mother's death.[8]

Sarah's story shows us that even faithful hearts can make regrettable mistakes. Her most serious lapse in judgment was in the Hagar matter. Because of her mistake, Isaac's descendants (the Jews) and Ishmael's descendants (the Arabs) have been at war throughout the ages. Still, the Bible highly regards Sarah as a faithful woman. Both Old and New Testament Scriptures extol her greatness as a matriarch.

As Abraham is "the father of all who believe,"[9] Sarah is surely their mother. The book of Hebrews includes Sarah as the first of two females in the cloud of faithful witnesses: "Through faith also Sarah herself received strength to conceive seed, and was delivered of a child when she was past age, because she judged him faithful who had promised" (Hebrews 11:11 KJV).

The apostle Peter, disregarding Sarah's outward beauty, praises her inner qualities and challenges all Christian women to be like her by excelling in the "unfading beauty of a gentle and quiet spirit."[10] He also distinguishes her as a model wife, citing her faithful submission to her husband. Indeed from the time she left Ur, she was with Abraham in her heart. Throughout her desert wanderings and her occasional errors in judgment, she carried good treasure in her heart that expressed itself in loving and sacrificial submission to her husband's interests. Peter calls women who follow her example "her daughters."[11]

## LESSONS FOR OUR HEARTS

*To the faithful you show yourself faithful. . . . Love the LORD, all his saints! The LORD preserves the faithful. . . . Let those who love the LORD hate evil, for he guards the lives of his faithful ones.*

PSALMS 18:25; 31:23; 97:10

I was certain God told me to marry my husband. The Holy Spirit said, "He's the one." I told my unbelieving dad, "I met the man I'm going to marry today, and when it happens, you'll know there's a God!" Although I was certain of the revelation, like Sarah, I felt pressure to do something to make it happen. Poor Sarah didn't trust God to provide a child apart from Hagar, and I didn't trust God to give me Clay apart from my own schemes.

As a new Christian, I had no idea how to simply trust God and wait on His timing. I worked fast and furious to win Clay's heart, and I got him. I was completely unrealistic in my expectations, believing that anything in God's will would mean smooth sailing—so why wait? We had known each other for just over two months when we got married. And even more quickly than that—while we were still on our honeymoon—the "honeymoon was over." I was shaking my fist at God, tearfully complaining, "You tricked me, God! I was supposed to live happily ever after!"

Clay and I had made some rude discoveries: We were as different as night and day; the only thing we had in common was that we loved God; and we were as strong-willed and stubborn as they come. Not surprisingly, our early years were filled with difficult adjustments.

One day, exasperated with the kind of life this marriage had dealt him, Clay heard from the Lord, who told him not to worry, to hang in there, and that I would be a good wife for him. By God's grace, as the years went by, we persevered to become survivors and conquerors. Life dealt us many serious ups, downs, twists, and turns, but we hung together like rocks in the surf rubbing and polishing each other smooth.

---

*For you need endurance, so that when you have done the will of God, you may receive what was promised.*

HEBREWS 10:36

---

Proverbs 31 speaks of the virtuous wife—a woman with whom I could certainly never compete. I particularly like the *New Revised Standard* rendering of verse 11, which says of this woman that "the heart of her husband trusts in her." One day, after some twenty years of marriage, Clay gave me the ultimate compliment before our congregation.

He said that no matter what happened in life, he knew he could always count on his wife, that I would always be there for him. This was a hallmark moment for me as I looked back at all the "near misses" of our lives. Who could have known the intensity of our upheavals? Who could have known the magnitude of our victory? Only Jesus.

Somehow through it all, God has forged in me a faithful heart on which Clay knows he can rely. Undergirding my faithfulness to my husband, however, was always the strong desire to remain faithful to God. I believed that to be faithful to God, I must obey Him, and that He wanted me to make this marriage succeed. I must not disgrace His name by failing at my marriage. I was in it for the long haul—"for better or for worse," "till death do us part."

When a Christian friend left her husband, saying, "I just don't love him anymore," I felt like screaming, "Love? It's a matter of your will!" I knew that feelings of love had not been the sustaining factor during the difficult years of our marriage. Feelings are fickle. At one time, filled with bitterness and despair, I hated the ground Clay walked on. However, after praying together and forgiving each other, I felt renewed hope, love, and respect for the man.

---

*But the fruit of the Spirit is . . . faithfulness. . . .*

GALATIANS 5:22

---

Faithfulness is what sustained our marriage—a commitment and resolve to honor God and not bring reproach on Him no matter what it might cost us personally. I do believe some marriages are "made in heaven" just as some lives seem to exhibit God's grace and beauty perpetually. Praise the Lord for these! But I am sure that many others, as with me, must expend lots of energy in praying, yielding, forgiving, and recommitting. While the promised blessing seems long in coming, I believe that the testimony of these faithful hearts is no less precious to the Lord.

We live in a society short on patience. We want instant everything. If a marriage isn't working, we want to trade it in as we would trade in our car. Worldly folks must have smirked recently to hear a Southern governor lamenting the sad fact that the Bible belt produced as many divorces among church people as among unchurched ones. How sad, in view of the Gospel's power! What disgrace God's Son must bear!

We must have faithful hearts—demonstrating faithfulness to our loved ones, to our friends, to our churches, and to God. How can we build this quality into our character? Perhaps it begins with realizing God's faithfulness to us. Just as "we love because He first loved us,"[12] we are faithful because we realize His faithfulness to us. We must believe that God loves us and keeps His promises to us.

While Sarah may not have seen it, God was faithful to her all along. He provided for her and protected her in all her travels, even protecting her from violation by foreign kings. But what about the promise she so desperately longed to see fulfilled? Between the promise and its fulfillment was a long period of waiting. We need to know two things about God: He is faithful to fulfill His promises, and He is always on schedule. By *His* clock, He is never late.

The long years of Sarah's disappointment over her barrenness, waiting each month to see if she might be pregnant—month after month, year after year, decade after decade—took their toll. We see in Sarah two coping mechanisms to which we, too, resort. First, she gave up believing God *could* fulfill His promise through her. So she thought He must need a backup plan and that she must help things along. Getting a surrogate to bear her child seemed a good solution, but it wasn't God's plan. Second, she gave up believing God *would* fulfill His promise through her. He had either changed His mind, or they had gotten their signals crossed. She did her best to fill the hole in her heart by dutifully serving her husband, her household, and her God. So hopeless was she about God's promise that when He finally came and said that it was time—she would experience motherhood at ninety years old!—she laughed.

Who would have thought Sarah could have a son at her great age? Who could have imagined she would live to raise him to adulthood? This should encourage us greatly. We, too, stumble around, wondering whether God is really with us. But if we maintain good treasure in our hearts, if we keep our hearts faithful, God will use our time of waiting and even our shortcomings and mistakes for great good. He will make of our tatters something beautiful.

---

*Be faithful, even to the point of death, and I will give you the crown of life. . . . This calls for patient endurance on the part of the saints who obey God's commandments and remain faithful to Jesus.*

REVELATION 2:10; 14:12

---

Faithful heart, are difficult obstacles challenging your faith? Are parts of your life on hold? Do you doubt, worry, and fear that God has forgotten you? Does it seem that His promises will never work for you? Don't give up; trust God; lean hard on His promises. Your wait is likely part of God's overarching plan for you. He often illustrates His omnipotence by waiting until we have exhausted our own resources. Through our waiting, God teaches us faith and patience. These are commodities we cannot purchase or earn. So don't try to take over for Him. Wait for Him; He will not fail you.

Miracles are standard procedure for our God. When He seems to ask of you the impossible, and you start to doubt His leading, remember Sarah and the question He put to her: "Is anything too hard for the Lord?" Never settle for an "Ishmael" when God has promised you "Isaac."

## Heart Check

1. How do you best relate to Sarah and her struggles?

2. What promise has God given you to claim that you are waiting to see fulfilled?

3. What steps can you take to ensure that your heart will remain faithful and true to the Lord and to your commitments?

4. What is the most important principle you can apply to your life from Sarah's example?

5. Compose a prayer to God in response to this chapter's lessons.

# 8

## Potiphar's Wife

### THE UNFAITHFUL HEART

GENESIS 39:6-20

OUTWARDLY SHE HAD IT ALL—everything other Egyptian women coveted. Wallowing in riches, living in a luxurious home with sundry servants, dining with royalty, Potiphar's wife knew that her slightest wish would be fulfilled. She was probably a vividly beautiful woman. As the wife of a high official with access to Pharaoh's courts and who even had Pharaoh's ear, she spent much of her time pampering herself, making sure she looked perfect. She must have been a sight with her stunning Egyptian features, including her lovely kohl-lined eyes, petal-soft skin, dark bejeweled hair, and voluptuous body lightly covered with silken garments. A truly sensational woman with the carriage and refinement of a queen, she was the type over whom men start revolutions.

Yet Potiphar's wife had something else going on inside her. Rich, spoiled, and bold, she got what she wanted—and she always wanted more. Behind the facade was a strong and turbulent woman, perhaps bored with her husband and consumed with reckless passion for fresh horizons. Yes, her awful heart impairment invited evil treasure and led her to disgrace her respected position.

Unlike faithful Sarah of whom we have never a hint of infidelity, Potiphar's wife cast her eyes on a young household servant, relentlessly pursuing him until her despicable story's end. She would not be worthy of mention in the Bible but for the fact that her object of lust was the upright man of God, Joseph. We call her heart The Unfaithful Heart, for she was an adulteress.

How did Joseph get into this fix? The story started when, as a seventeen-year-old, he was Jacob's favorite son. For this, his ten elder brothers hated him. The last straw came when the starry-eyed youth reported dreams to his brothers in which the family bowed down to him. Did he think he was God's favorite, too? His brothers despised him even more.

One day when Jacob sent Joseph to his brothers in the fields, their jealousy overtook them. They said to each other, "Here comes that dreamer. . . . Let's kill him!" They would have done it, too, but for the intervention of the eldest brother, Reuben. Instead, they sold Joseph to a passing caravan of Midianite merchants going to Egypt. In Egypt the merchants sold Joseph to Potiphar. As the captain of the guard,[1] he was the head of palace bodyguards, prison wardens, and executioners. Joseph would have good reason to watch his p's and q's in this man's house!

Everything had changed for Joseph. His life as a nomadic shepherd boy living in a tent among grazing animals was now history. The Egypt in which he landed was a highly civilized and organized empire. Because Potiphar was extremely wealthy, Joseph would not live shabbily. His Egyptian home was likely an elaborate two- or three-story dwelling with balconies and lavish gardens, stables, and fields. It had brightly painted interior walls and ceilings. The master and his family dined in style with live entertainment and rich foods served on elegant gold tableware. The lavishly decorated home featured alabaster vases, ceramic pots, exquisite rugs, expensive paintings, and beautifully designed hand-carved furniture evincing a fastidious, elegant lifestyle.

Despite Joseph's personal trauma, he loved God and resolved to walk with Him in this strange land where he was no longer a boy spoiled by his doting father, but a slave. Living in Potiphar's mansion, he must be clean-shaven, dress like an Egyptian, and learn the language and culture. He adapted quickly.

Keeping a large and impressive household running smoothly takes skill. Since Potiphar disliked details, he left many things undone. They began to come together, however, when Joseph entered his service. Potiphar soon realized he had "struck it rich" in buying the young slave. Joseph proved to be an organizational genius, and his honesty, integrity, loyalty, and devotion to duty all deeply impressed his master.

While Potiphar did not know Joseph's God, he appreciated the success this God gave the industrious youth. Shortly, such a relationship of mutual respect grew between the two men that Potiphar promoted Joseph above his other slaves. As his attendant, Joseph had charge of everything Potiphar owned. With his keen wisdom and steadfast loyalty, he was worth his weight in gold: "From the time he put him in charge . . . the LORD blessed the household of the Egyptian because of Joseph. The blessing of the LORD was on everything Potiphar had, both in the house and in the field" (Genesis 39:5).

Managing the sizeable property kept the young overseer busy. Potiphar never worried about a thing in his entire household. He trusted Joseph so implicitly that he no longer bothered even to check on his affairs. He only concerned himself with the food he ate, and this only because he chose to.

This is where Potiphar's wife enters the story. Perhaps her husband's interest in food superseded his interest in her. Their relationship definitely lacked something, and she had her own appetites. With so many servants doing her bidding, she was likely bored with too little to do. So she went looking for an amorous adventure, probably not her first.

Like Potiphar, she was impressed with Joseph's brightness, diligence, and eagerness to serve. He was also "well-built and handsome," and she could not help noticing it. Indeed he no longer looked like the scruffy Hebrew shepherd boy who first entered her house. Now, standing erect and confident, he had a great presence, born of certainty in his relationship with God.

His mistress admired Joseph's serious, dedicated face. His features were as beautifully sculpted as her own. Gleaming trimmed hair framed his handsome face; a deep colorful collar of fine embroidery and beadwork punctuated his muscular torso; a short pleated linen skirt tucked into his leather belt showed off his sinuous legs. Increasingly fixating on the handsome young male specimen, she slipped into fantasies that suddenly gave her life fresh color. She knew him to be a man of high moral character, but that only fueled her passion.

Joseph probably lived in servants' quarters somewhere on the first floor while his master and his family lived upstairs. As the young man grew in prominence and was increasingly on his own, he had freedom to move up and down the stairs at will. The woman's dark, watchful eyes flickered with excitement each time she saw him coming. With warmth, she would saunter up to him, lick her painted lips, and perhaps say, "Joseph, you're doing such a fine job. How can I *ever* thank you. If you need *anything*, well . . . just remember, I'm here for you, Joseph."

Joseph was no doubt a gentleman who treated his master's wife politely, but he could not help noticing her undue interest in him. He never encouraged her, but she did not need it. He became fearfully aware of the meaningful glances she flashed at him, the playful smiles. Egyptian women, unlike Hebrew women, painted their faces, wore sheer linen fabrics, and left their heads and arms bare. Hebrews wore no makeup, used rough fabrics, and covered themselves up. And this Egyptian was *so* sensual. How could a healthy young man not feel the power of her seduction? Joseph struggled to keep his eyes down.

As for Potiphar, we can assume that as a high-ranking official, his duties took him away from home often. Day after day his lonely wife stared at the handsome young Hebrew. Perhaps she was experiencing midlife crisis and wanted to prove she still had what it takes. It is also possible, but not probable, that Potiphar was a eunuch. (The Hebrew word for "official"[2] used to describe him, *cariyc,* can also be translated eunuch.) Still, from what we see in the story, he was a faithful and caring husband.

Whatever the source of her discontent, this woman had no excuse for her unfaithful heart. And what she was doing to her virtuous young servant was reprehensible. She could have admired his inner virtue and been impressed with his God, as was her husband. She could have asked Joseph about his God. God always lets honest seekers find Him; He delights to fill empty hearts. But she wanted just one thing—to have sex with Joseph.

Potiphar's wife and Joseph had nothing in common. She was rich and powerful; he was a slave. She was an Egyptian; he was a Hebrew. She was married; he was single. She was older; he was a youth. She was an adulteress; he was virtuous. She served herself; he honored God. Perhaps all these differences made the challenge even more appealing to her. She must have been driven, constantly eyeing him with burning lust.

One day she decided to fully unveil her unfaithful heart in a bold move. "Send Joseph to my room; I want to see him at once!" she likely commanded a servant. Hurrying to her room, she perfumed it and herself, checked her makeup, and then draped herself sumptuously across the satiny pillows on her bed and waited.

---

*"I have decked my couch with coverings, colored spreads of Egyptian linen; I have perfumed my bed with myrrh, aloes, and cinnamon. Come, let us take our fill of love until morning, let us delight ourselves with love. For my husband is not at home; he has gone on a long journey." . . . And now, my children, listen to me, and be attentive to the words of my mouth. Do not let your hearts turn aside to her ways; do not stray into her paths. For many are those she has laid low, and numerous are her victims.*

PROVERBS 7:16-19, 24-26 NRSV

---

Joseph's heart and his eyes must have dropped as he entered the room. Her sensuous face was firmly set on him, direct and challenging. With a toss of her head, she demanded, "Come to bed with me!"

What a flattering and powerful temptation for a virile young man! While her invitation was hideous, it was also alluring. Her husband was gone, they were alone, she was attractive and eager. Yet adultery was as wrong in Egyptian culture as anywhere else and even a serious crime. Joseph blinked in astonished dread. Perhaps she urged him, "Come on, Joseph, no one will ever know; it will be our secret."

The thought of violating his master's trust appalled Joseph. He deeply respected this man who had trusted him implicitly with all he owned and elevated him to an esteemed position. Perhaps other slaves before him had succumbed to this siren's beauty and sexual agility. But hers was no "bed of roses." She not only had their bodies, but she had their souls. Outwardly Joseph may have been a slave, but he was bent on remaining inwardly free.

He tried not to offend her with his refusal. "With me in charge," he told her, "my master does not concern himself with anything in the house; everything he owns he has entrusted to my care. No one is greater in this house than I am. My master has withheld nothing from me except you, because you are his wife. How then could I do such a wicked thing and sin against God?" (Genesis 39:7-9).

He had it right. Sexual sin is not just a matter between two consenting adults; it is "sin against God." Perhaps no one else would ever have known about their sinful adultery, but God would have.

Potiphar's wife drew an astonished breath at the young upstart's refusal. Her face fell in disappointment. "Oh, Joseph!" she may have pouted sensuously. As he nervously backed out of the room, she had a wounded look in her eyes—but it was no look of defeat. She had the confidence level of a lioness. This reticent young man would give up his scruples soon enough. So with obsessive devotion to her mission, she kept hounding him, trying hard to break his will: "She spoke to Joseph day after day."

Joseph did not know what to do. His well-ordered life had turned chaotic. He could handle any household crisis but this. Surely he spent many hours praying for a solution. As he raced about his duties, the only glances he gave his nemesis were quick, denying ones. "He refused to go to bed with her or even be with her."

Finally Potiphar's wife, tired of this cat-and-mouse game, decided to pounce on her victim. Poor Joseph. The record says, "One day he went into the house to attend to his duties, and none of the household servants was inside." None? Hmm. Hard to imagine who was responsible for that!

Suddenly there she was, an electric look in her lustful eyes. Joseph, however, saw only death in those bright eyes. Perhaps she thought that if she could get him in her arms just once, her charms would overcome him. She reached out to grab him, but he stepped back.

"She caught him by his cloak and said, 'Come to bed with me!'" He desperately tried to pull himself loose, but she had a firm grip. So "he left his cloak in her hand and ran out of the house." Cloak? Don't get the wrong idea. The Hebrew word *beged* is translated garment, clothes, or raiment. Joseph likely tore from the house wearing a mere loincloth! Still, the embarrassment he felt as he ran past other servants was worth it. He fled from the femme fatale not as a coward, but to honor his God and his master and to preserve his integrity.

Now what? Joseph's resistance had finally burst all the bubbles in her pretty little head. Would she let herself be denied—by a slave? As the proverb says, "Hell hath no fury like a woman scorned"— especially a wicked woman. Those playful eyes became black holes against her face—hard, fierce, and pitiless. A smile crawled to her lips, curving like a poisonous snake. She knew what to do with the incriminating evidence in her hand, lest it be used against her.

"When she saw that he had left his cloak in her hand and had run out of the house, she called her household servants." Her face was red and blotchy, and she trembled with anger as she spewed out her concocted story: "Look, this Hebrew has been brought to us to make sport of us! He came in here to sleep with me, but I screamed."

Really! The servants may have looked at each other curiously, wondering, "I didn't hear any screams. Did you?" The lady was shrewd, though, appealing to their own latent resentment toward Joseph as a foreigner undeservedly elevated above them by their master. She had fought the wicked foreigner off, not only for herself, but for them all. He had disgraced the entire household—"us."

With the grace of a killer shark, she held up the circumstantial evidence and went on: "When he heard me scream for help, he left his cloak beside me and ran out of the house." We have no evidence that they really believed her. They probably knew both Joseph and their mistress better than that. Yet they would not dare challenge her story. After this dress rehearsal, she prepared for the real performance when Potiphar got home.

Potiphar entered the house and could tell immediately that something was wrong. He could feel tension in the air. His servants nervously greeted him, but Joseph was nowhere in sight. His wife stormed in, demanding to see him privately. As he followed her into a room, everyone could hear her high-pitched cry as she repeated her story: "That Hebrew slave you brought us came to me to make sport of me. But as soon as I screamed for help, he left his cloak beside me and ran out of the house." What a noble woman—a real heroine!

How did Potiphar respond? "When his master heard the story his wife told him, saying, 'This is how your slave treated me,' he burned with anger."

This woman is smooth. Did you hear her suggest that not only was it Joseph's fault but Potiphar's? "That Hebrew slave *you* brought us. . . . This is how *your* slave treated me." This tactic put increased pressure on Potiphar to act against Joseph. After all, his decision to give the young man such authority and freedom had not only endangered her but the entire household.

Potiphar could imagine the scene: Joseph sneaking up on his poor wife, grabbing her, trying to ravish her, demanding that she not tell a soul. He could see her gasping and valiantly screaming, flailing, and nobly fighting him off, keeping her wits about her enough to grab his cloak as evidence. As he cradled his distressed wife in his arms, apologizing for jeopardizing her, he was furious.

But wait! Didn't Potiphar stop and wonder about the veracity of this story as he thought of his wife's character and then Joseph's? It seems he did. He could have had Joseph executed that very night. He had executed many for similar crimes, and this is certainly the outcome his wife hoped to see. But "Joseph's master took him and put him in prison, the place where the king's prisoners were confined." As chief warden of Egypt's prisons, Potiphar got Joseph a milder penalty and sent him to a royal prison rather than one for common criminals (Genesis 39:10-20).

Regardless, it must have stung the young man deeply who had already suffered such rejection from his own family. Now a man he deeply respected had accused him and judged him guilty of an abhorrent crime he had never committed. Meanwhile, the one who assassinated his reputation got off scot-free. What grief Joseph must have felt as he was forced from the home he had served with excellence and put into a dreary prison.

---

*It [wisdom] will save you also from the adulteress, from the wayward wife with her seductive words, who has left the partner of her youth and ignored the covenant she made before God. . . . For the lips of an adulteress drip honey, and her speech is smoother than oil; but in the end she is bitter as gall, sharp as a double-edged sword. Her feet go down to death; her steps lead straight to the grave. She gives no thought to the way of life; her paths are crooked, but she knows it not.*

PROVERBS 2:16-17; 5:3-6

---

Yes, Joseph was cast into prison that day, and Potiphar's wife had her revenge. But she would always know her guilt, Joseph would know his innocence, and God would eventually bring justice. While we do not know what subsequently transpired in this despicable woman's life—she fades into obscurity—we do know that the ultimate loss was hers, not Joseph's. He had risen from his previous personal tragedy, and, as cream rises to the top, he would triumph through this misfortune, too.

Potiphar's wife had the potential for doing much good. Instead she wasted her life. She rubbed shoulders with one who was destined to become one of history's great men. She could have taken note of the good treasure in him and sought it for her own heart. How tragic that instead of learning from him, she tried to corrupt him. She could have turned from temptation as he did, but refusing to curb her desires, she invited sin to consume her instead. God's Spirit had come to her house with Joseph, and her entire household was blessed. How terrible that she chased the blessing away by entertaining an unfaithful heart. Ultimately she wickedly condemned Joseph, an innocent man. History has nothing good to say of her.

Joseph, on the other hand, maintained his virtue and with God's favor went on to emerge as governor of all Egypt, second only to Pharaoh. When he became Egypt's ruler, he became the ruler over Potiphar's wife, too. We can only imagine the shame, guilt, and fear of retribution she lived with until the end of her days.

## LESSONS FOR OUR OWN HEARTS

Adultery bears bitter fruit. Just look at Potiphar's wife. What began as flirting with sin turned deadly. Not love, but hatred consumed her disappointed, unfaithful heart. Thus she piled her sins ever higher. God's Word says, "There are six things the LORD hates, seven that are detestable to him: haughty eyes, a lying tongue, hands that shed inno-cent blood, a heart that devises wicked schemes, feet that are quick to rush into evil, a false witness who pours out lies, and a man who stirs up dissension among brothers" (Proverbs 6:16-19). Of which was she innocent? An unfaithful heart is a devastating impairment indeed!

A woman given to an unfaithful heart probably does not simply wake up one day and embrace this approach to life. She does not just step outside to get her newspaper, blink at the sunshine, and say, "My, what a lovely day to commit adultery!" On the contrary, such a condi-tion starts as a tiny and yet pernicious virus in the heart that ruins her because she misjudged the danger. The Bible charges us, "Above all else, guard your heart, for it is the wellspring of life" (Proverbs 4:23).

I well remember how the virus once began to infect my heart. I worked at the local City Hall in the City Clerk's office. The various department counters encircled a wide marble floor. One day I noticed the handsome building inspector across the expanse staring at me from the Building Department. Immediately something flashed in my soul, like light caught in water. He smoothly smiled and looked away. The intensity of his vibes stunned me. It happened again the next day. Only this time our eyes met, a message was given and received, an agreement was made. The transaction was done in a moment with our eyes, and when they had separated, I knew I was in trouble. We had begun a flirting relationship across the hall.

For days this went on. Each day I was alive with anticipatory adrenaline as I waited to exchange smiles. I knew it was wrong and that I must deal with it, but I just wanted to toy with the sin a bit longer. God bore down on my conscience, however, and I knew what I must do. Since my heart was under assault, I needed help. I went home and confessed it to Clay, and we prayed through it together.

I went to work the next day, and there he was. This was the day he had intended to take the game to the next level. As he moseyed over to my area, I instinctively knew this was it. With his dreamy smile, he said, "Hi." I returned a curt "hello" and pretended to go back to work on my stack of papers. I knew that in that instant I had cut the thing off; it had ended as quickly as it had begun. As he stomped away, I felt no thrill of victory; in fact, I felt as if I had self-destructively hacked myself. Indeed I had landed a painful blow to my sinful flesh.

I still wished to have a civil atmosphere between us, but God did not allow it. He could see that my heart was not yet perfectly clean as I secretly grieved a bit for my lost playmate. Our eyes never again met, and my heart's sinful virus died. Perhaps my little escapade doesn't sound like much to you, but it was to me. I felt its power; I knew its seriousness. Entering a forbidden path is never trivial.

It is easy to be like the proverbial monkey whose owner said, "If you eat any of those bananas in that banana tree, you'll be shot!" The owner left, and the little guy stared up at those luscious bananas. "I won't eat a banana; I just want to get a closer look," he told himself. As he started up the tree, he said, "Oh, I just want to smell them; but I won't eat any." As he drew near and could smell them, he just wanted to touch one. Upon touching one, he just wanted to peel it, and finally he just wanted to wrap his tongue around it. Suddenly before he could think about it, the banana was down his throat, and you know what happened to the monkey!

Each day we make choices in our hearts either to obey God and resist evil or to give in to ungodly, corrupting influences. In today's culture nearly everyone is touched either directly or indirectly by the problem of adultery. Television, movies, magazines, and novels spew it forth, convincing us that traditional prohibitions are no longer carved in stone, that the church must adjust its outmoded thinking to faddish cultural values. Sexual infidelity is the norm in Hollywood, and the average American absorbs about four hours daily of its sinful sermonizing.

Not long ago a contemporary Christian music diva ran off with the man of her dreams. Unfortunately, it meant destroying two marriages. Years of counseling had never solved the conflicts in her heart and home, so finally she gave it up and went with her heart. At last she and her lover got what they wanted, likely counting it a triumph of love, knowing how quickly their forgiving fans would let the dust settle. Still, in my book they tragically went down in flames for all the smirking world to see and talk about. As I read about it in *People* magazine, I felt ashamed that she was not just anyone—she was supposedly God's child, representing God's church.

Divorce because of infidelity is not uncommon in Christian circles. What is surprising is the sense of "rightness" people have when they "fall in love" with another. While most said their wedding vows with all sincerity, they must not have thought deeply about them. Perhaps they were certain nothing could ever tempt them to break their vows because they would never feel differently. They would always be "in love," right?

What we fail to understand is that we do not exchange our vows as expressions of our feelings but of our commitment to faithfulness—no matter the direction our feelings fly. How easily we can lend sacred approval to infidelity because "things just didn't work out" and because this time we are "*really* in love." The guilty cheaters may think their love will last forever. Yet Eros, the pagan god of love before whose altar they have knelt, is untrustworthy. He will degrade and consume them until they fully discover the rotten fruit of their adultery—guilt, frustration, anger, suspicion, alienation, and more of the loneliness that drove them to sin in the first place.

How can we guard our hearts against unfaithfulness? First, we must preserve our loyalty to God. He is entirely faithful to us. He keeps His vows and has promised, "Never will I leave you; never will I forsake you" (Hebrews 13:5). We can count on Him, and His faithfulness demands ours in return. We cannot be faithful to God and unfaithful to our spouse at the same time: "Therefore what *God* has joined together, let man not separate" (Mark 10:9).

We need Joseph's perspective toward sin: "How then could I do such a wicked thing and sin against God?" The Law of Moses was not yet given in Joseph's time. But he knew from oral tradition and his own conscience that adultery is sin—great sin against God and His moral nature. Joseph was right. Every immoral act of sexual intercourse outside marriage is a sin that God abhors. How much less excuse have we who possess the entire Bible!

If we cannot stay faithful for love, then we should do it for fear. Christians drop like flies, falling from grace to disgrace, when they take God's grace as a license to live disobedient lifestyles. Just a reminder: "Thou shalt not commit adultery" (Exodus 20:14 KJV) is the seventh of the Ten *Commandments*, and it is no more a mere suggestion now than when God first gave it. People today have lost their sense of accountability to God; they have no fear of His displeasure. Thus immorality is rampant.

What else can you do? Here are a few ideas:

*Totally* commit yourself to faithfulness to your husband, whether he be an earthly one or the heavenly One.

Be patient with the process of building a strong marriage.

Anticipate danger and plan a way of escape. Before any attack, you should build your hedges.

Beware of self-deception. It's easy to take one step and then another down the road of rationalization.

Don't be naive. We are all susceptible to sexual sin, so don't presume you and your marriage are invulnerable.

Pray with your spouse for your marriage.

When tempted, humble yourself, confess your need, and get prayer.

Avoid temptation. Recognize the traps, remove the stumbling blocks, send temptation away when it comes knocking. If you need to, run from it.

Love your husband; don't give Satan a foothold by harboring anger and bitterness; destroy any evil virus in your heart by forgiving and thinking loving thoughts about him.

> *In the same way, count yourselves dead to sin but alive to God in Christ*
> *Jesus. Therefore do not let sin reign in your mortal body so that you obey*
> *its evil desires. Do not offer the parts of your body to sin, as instruments*
> *of wickedness, but rather offer yourselves to God, as those who have*
> *been brought from death to life; and offer the parts of your body to him*
> *as instruments of righteousness.*
>
> ROMANS 6:11-13

We must restore the virtue of faithfulness in our generation. Adultery is ruining marriages, children, churches, and our nation. God calls us as Christians to renounce worldly values and fill our hearts with the good treasures of His righteousness. Then we can be lights, showing the world a better way. At the same time, if you have ever succumbed to this sin, there is a way out. God has grace and forgiveness for you. If you have repented, you need not live with guilt forever. Guilt over an affair plagued one elderly woman for more than fifty years. God does not want you to live like this, for "there is now no condemnation for those who are in Christ Jesus" (Romans 8:1).

### Heart Check

1. Comparing Sarah's faithful heart and the adulterous heart of Potiphar's wife, how can you cultivate a faithful heart and guard against an adulterous one?

2. In what ways do you think the secular world has influenced your values concerning sexual morality? Do you detect unfaithful attitudes in your heart?

3. Are there specific actions the Holy Spirit would have you take to cleanse your heart?

4. What is the most important principle you can apply to your life from the example of Potiphar's wife?

5. Compose a prayer in response to this chapter's lessons.

# 9

## THE UNDIVIDED HEART

MARK 14:3-9; LUKE 10:38-42; JOHN 11:1-45; 12:1-8

TWO MILES OUTSIDE JERUSALEM on the eastern slope of the Mount of Olives sat the quiet little village of Bethany, home to three very special people: a woman named Mary, her sister Martha, and their brother Lazarus. These three were dear friends to the Lord Jesus Christ.

Mary and Martha shared a home that because of its proximity to Jerusalem was a convenient place for Jesus to lodge. The One who had "nowhere to lay His head"[1] no doubt deeply appreciated their open invitation of hospitality and stayed with them more than a few times.[2]

Of His Bethany friends, Mary in particular is noted for her remarkable heart of uncluttered devotion to Jesus. In fact, we see in Mary a heart drawn to Him with a unique passion. We call her heart The Undivided Heart. Single in purpose and wholly reserved for Jesus, it receives and holds kingdom treasure and keeps hungering and thirsting for more. No matter what went on around her, Mary's heart stayed firmly fixed on Jesus Christ.

---

*Teach me your way, O LORD, and I will walk in your truth; give me an undivided heart, that I may fear your name.*

PSALM 86:11

---

We see Mary on three occasions in Scripture. In all three, we find her at Jesus' feet in humble worship and adoration. Let's visit this lovely woman of God so we can better understand the type of heart that touches God's own heart.

One day when Jesus and His disciples were passing through the area, Jesus stopped in at Mary and Martha's house. How different in temperament are these two sisters who love Jesus. Mary is more reflective than her busy sister, and on this occasion their differences clash. A gifted and organized hostess who felt deeply honored by the disciples' visit, Martha wanted everything just so that day. Things were not going as planned, however, and she felt the pressure.

One thing elevating Martha's blood pressure was Mary's seeming insensitivity to the pressing household needs. There Mary was, lazily sitting with the men, listening to Jesus instead of helping her prepare the meal. Martha couldn't even tap her on the shoulder, since Mary had plopped herself right up front at Jesus' feet. There was no way to get her attention without making a scene.

Martha was not only upset with Mary, but she was also frustrated with the Lord for allowing Mary to get away with it. *Neither of them cares about* my *needs*, she probably thought. Finally, no longer able to conceal her aggravation, she burst in on the peaceful front-room discussion: "Lord, don't you care that my sister has left me to do the work by myself? Tell her to help me" (Luke 10:40).

Before going on, we should again note Jesus' radical affirmation of women. Here He challenges traditional Jewish role distinctions between men and women. While people normally sat on chairs or reclined on couches when in someone's home, a dedicated disciple would sit at His teacher's feet—as Mary was doing. Her posture and her earnestness to absorb Jesus' teaching would seem scandalous to most Jewish men. As a rule, Jewish men thanked God in their prayers every morning for not creating them as slaves, heathen, or women. But Jesus welcomed Mary to sit at His feet and learn along with the other disciples. This would be especially surprising since disciples were in training for taking on leadership roles, something not at all culturally acceptable for women of that day.

Leaving Martha to function as hostess, the expected female role on such an occasion, Mary seized her opportunity to learn with the men. We don't see in her a woman striving for emancipation from a male-dominated society. No, her real motive was love for Jesus. In Him her life took on bright new hues. She saw previously undreamed-of possibilities for her life, felt unprecedented value, purpose, and meaning. For Jesus loved her and filled her heart with wondrous kingdom treasure. She felt significant; she could carry herself with dignity never before known to her. He treated her with the respect afforded a disciple. For Mary, life itself had become Jesus Christ.

With Christ, Mary lost all track of time and responsibility. She sat enthralled at His feet, hanging on His divine words of life, pressing in to know and understand Him better. With a heart wholly His, an undivided heart, she forgot other pursuits. Food? Physical food could never satisfy the way Jesus' words did. Preparing a feast? This WAS a feast. Although Martha failed to see it, food was the last thing on Jesus' mind. He once said His food was to do the will of Him who sent Him. Mary recognized that He was far more concerned right then with this "food" than with any they could serve Him.

Was Mary in any way being inhospitable to Jesus? Of course not. An inhospitable person would pay little attention to her guest. Did the Lord come to their house because He could get great meals there or because He could find great companionship? Clearly, being with people was His priority. He never let creature comforts interfere with His mission to reach people's hearts.

How did Jesus respond to Martha's frustrated demand? "Martha, Martha," He sighed, "you are worried and upset about many things, but only one thing is needed. Mary has chosen what is better, and it will *not* be taken away from her" (Luke 10:42).

Ouch! Jesus identified Mary as the sensitive one, the one who was making the far better choice. Let's be clear in saying, however, that just because Mary refused this time to follow her sister's lead in the kitchen does not mean she never served. It simply means that Martha needed to learn something from her sister about sensitivity to Jesus. Mary was not just following her own wishes; she was doing exactly what He wanted of her. He *wanted* to fill the treasure chest of her heart with more of His kingdom treasure that day, and Mary's duty to Him superseded her duty to Martha.

It would be wrong to think that Mary was passive while her sister was active. Mary expresses her devotion by actively choosing the better part. While she never even speaks in this incident, her language is one of the heart. She did not need to defend herself—Jesus did it for her. Jesus will always defend an undivided heart for Him.

We see again on another occasion Mary's undivided heart in the emotionally charged story of Lazarus, her brother. A crisis hit the Bethany family when what was perhaps a minor illness for Lazarus suddenly turned serious. Desperate, the sisters sought Jesus for help. He was ministering at the time in Galilee on the other side of the Jordan River, a long journey from Bethany. They sent a messenger to inform Him of their crisis, saying, "Lord, the one you love is ill."

Although the sisters gave no specific request for Him to come, they expected Jesus to do the right thing for the one He loved. But when Jesus heard their message, he did not seem alarmed at all. In fact, He brushed it off, saying, "This sickness will not end in death." Then he added, "No, it is for God's glory so that God's Son may be glorified through it" (John 11:3-4). While He loved His friends, He decided to stay in Galilee for another two days.

Meanwhile, back in Bethany Lazarus' condition was worsening. We can imagine the urgent questions swimming around in his sisters' minds: *Why did this have to happen to our brother now? Why did Jesus have to be away? Will He get the message in time? Will He understand the urgency? Why doesn't He get here?* Then they would reassure themselves: *Certainly Jesus will do what needs to be done—just as He always does.*

We can see the two distressed sisters—Martha bent over her brother, caring for him, and Mary staring out the window anxiously yearning: *If only Jesus would get here.* But Lazarus died. He probably even died before their messenger reached Jesus.

The sisters were grief-stricken. Martha, the stronger and more task-oriented of the two, probably bore up better as she made preparation for the burial, which in that climate usually followed the death by one day. Sensitive Mary, on the other hand, must have kept wondering about Jesus, sobbing her heart out, "Why, oh, why? Where is Jesus? Why didn't He get here? He healed multitudes whom He didn't even know. This was Lazarus, His friend. Oh, Jesus, where are You? I need You so badly."

The messenger returned home—alone. Not only did Jesus not get there to pray for His dying friend, but neither did He make it for the burial. In fact, He did not get there till after Mary and Martha had been grieving for four days. This must have been an excruciating disappointment to the sisters. How could they understand that despite His closeness to them, He could not allow external forces to supersede the Father's will. Finally—although His disciples feared going because of hostile Jews in the area—they set out for Judea.

In Jewish culture the first week for grieving a close relative was spent in deep mourning in one's house, sitting on the floor and being visited by friends. This custom, called shivah, lasted seven days, the first three of which were days of weeping. During this time the sisters could not wash, wear shoes, study, or transact business. Surely during those days of mourning with friends and neighbors, the sisters had lots of time to ponder their perplexing questions. When someone asked, "Where's Jesus? Doesn't He care?" Mary probably replied, "Of course He cares; He has His reasons." Her undivided heart never stopped believing in His love, even while it asked why.

After what seemed an eternity, Martha heard that Jesus was coming. She ran to meet Him and received His consolation. Then to make sure Mary got a few minutes alone with Him before the crowds engulfed them, she went back and called Mary aside, telling her that Jesus was there and wanted to see her. Not wasting a moment, Mary flew out of the house, a train of mourners following her.

Mary, far more emotional and tender than her sister, was overcome with grief. A broken heart, however, does not mean a divided heart. Jesus was still her heart's treasure. In an act of homage and a confession of faith, she fell at His feet, a humble expression of her heart's submission to His will—whatever it might be. She did this in the presence of a whole crowd of mourners, many of whom she knew were not His friends. She felt no shame or fear to fall at His feet. "Lord," she sobbed, "if You had been here, my brother would not have died."

Mary only said these few words, the same words her sister had said before her, but what she was lacking in words, she made up for with intensity. Lazarus had died, and Jesus had come to raise him. Yet even Jesus was not prepared for the surge of emotion that hit Him. Mary's tears spoke loudly enough to wrench His heart.

Why the depth of emotion? Did He grieve as He saw the beauty of Mary's undivided heart? What a contrast with the stubborn, unbelieving, critical hearts of many Jews standing there with her. Did He feel the pain of His own cup of suffering that would so soon cause Mary's heart to break again? Did He think of the heartache that sin and death had brought to a world of people He loved? Tears began to spill down His cheeks. The mourners—probably noisy and demonstrative—provided an even more emotionally poignant backdrop. Weeping openly, the Son of God asked, "Where have you laid him?"

Arriving at the tomb, He was still groaning in grief. He commanded that the stone covering the tomb's entrance be removed. He prayed to His Father and then forcefully called, "Lazarus, come out!" (John 11:32-44). And Lazarus, wrapped in grave clothes, appeared in the opening!

Lazarus' illness and death had been Mary's major "crisis-of-belief" experience. She had wondered why Jesus had not come to their aid more quickly. She had felt so alone and forgotten. Now she understood. She would never again question Him. Aglow with passionate love for the awesome and wonderful Lord who had called her brother back from death, she gave Jesus her whole heart.

The raising of Lazarus after four days was an incredible miracle that would begin a chain of events leading to Christ's death. After news of the miracle got to the Pharisees, they began serious consultations about how best to destroy Him. Meanwhile Jesus knew He could no longer move about publicly. He withdrew instead to a region near the desert.

Six days before the Passover, Jesus returned to Bethany, for what would be His final visit.[3] The chief priests and Pharisees had given orders that anyone finding Jesus should report it so they might arrest Him. Knowing this, His friends decided to honor Jesus with a festive but private Sabbath meal. Simon the Leper, likely healed by Jesus, offered to host the event.[4]

As always, Mary watched the Lord carefully. She had developed deep spiritual insight while sitting at His feet. Studying Him during this visit, she must have perceived signs of strain in His face. No one else noticed, but she discerned the heaviness and sorrow in His heart. He had spoken often of the sufferings He must soon endure. She knew of the hatred of His enemies, first simmering and now boiling. They talked not only of killing the Lord but of killing her brother along with Him.

*Oh, the pain in my Lord's heart!* she thought. *Is there something I might do for Him? Does He have some special need? May I honor Him in some way?* God gave Mary a revelation. Did she understand the full significance of it? Probably not. But an idea formed in her mind. She knew exactly what she would do.[5]

The men did not really notice Mary slip into the room that night. They were busy eating and talking. If they noticed her at all, they probably thought she was serving the meal along with her sister Martha. But Mary had again left her sister to do the serving. Quietly waiting for the right moment, she stole up to Jesus and knelt at His feet. Because the men often had seen her sit at their Master's feet, they still paid her no attention. Suddenly, however, Mary took an alabaster flask out from between the folds of her garment. She felt no shyness as she carefully took the lid off the bottle.

Mary's bottle contained perfumed oil—pure nard imported from India's Himalaya Mountains. It was of highest quality and therefore very expensive. She had probably kept it as a family treasure, her most precious possession. Its value approximated the annual wages of a common laborer—a lifetime's savings! But when it came to Jesus, Mary never even counted the cost. Her love was as pure as her precious ointment. Love like this gives everything and only regrets it has not more to give.

She tenderly poured the perfume out over Jesus' feet, the feet that soon would be pierced for her sins. There was nothing typical about her action. Since this kind of pure nard was often used to anoint kings, she may have intentionally been anointing Jesus to declare her loyalty to Him as her King and Messiah. However, anointing oil was always poured on the head, not the feet. Water alone was provided for feet, never oil, and it was the lowest slave in a household who did the washing. Mary's act of pouring it on Christ's feet was an act of utter humility. It was an extreme act of worship from an undivided heart. Holding nothing back, as if pouring forth her very soul, Mary poured it all out, an entire pint of it. She said nothing. No words would have sufficed to express her feelings.

Mary had not intended to make a scene. She had planned to slip in and out quietly. But the sweet-smelling oil poured out over Jesus' precious feet eluded no one's notice. Everything came to a stop; the room fell silent. In a striking move, Mary let down her hair and tenderly began to wipe the Lord's feet with it.

This is striking in that a Jewish woman never unbound her hair in public, apparently being a mark of loose morals. But Mary did not stop to consider public reaction; her love for Jesus was stronger than social convention. Forgetting everyone else, her heart wholly focused on the Lord and ministering to His troubled heart. The fragrant beauty of the perfume—and of the moment— permeated the entire house.

What happened next was like someone throwing a bucket of paint on a masterpiece. Jesus' own disciples, clueless as to the depth and beauty of this moment, became indignant at Mary's extravagance. Grumbling and complaining, they asked each other, "Why this *waste*?" How out of touch with God's heart they were. They were still too absorbed in their thoughts of coming glory to perceive the truth.

The disciples believed in Jesus; they followed Jesus; they thought Jesus was the Messiah. But they did not yet love like this. Acting like legalistic Pharisees, full of self-righteous indignation, they began to rebuke Mary harshly.

One disciple—the group's treasurer—knew the oil's value, to be sure. While other disciples complained, Judas burned with anger. "Why wasn't this perfume sold and the money given to the poor?"[6] he demanded. Judas did not really care about the poor. He kept the money bag and helped himself to its contents now and then. His question merely exposed his heart, which reeked of greed, covetousness, and dishonesty. He cloaked his sinful heart by citing practicality and principle. Yet since when is love practical? Does not love sometimes make us do crazy, extravagant things?

How could Judas understand a heart of undivided devotion, a heart in love? While Jesus had never moved away from him, Judas had already moved away from Jesus in his heart. Paradoxically, following this incident, Judas ran out and betrayed his Lord for thirty pieces of silver, a fraction of the value of Mary's gift.

We can see Mary crushed and broken by her accusers, kneeling before Jesus' feet, looking up into His eyes seeking reassurance. As when Mary's sister misinterpreted her actions and Jesus defended her, we again see Jesus coming to her defense. "Leave her alone," He ordered. "It was intended that she should save this perfume for the day of my burial. You will always have the poor among you, but you will not always have me" (John 12:7-8).

While Jewish kings and priests were anointed for service, the Lord signifies that this anointing was different—an anointing for burial. He knew He must soon make His dreadful journey to the cross, and this remark reveals how heavily it weighed on His heart. This is the only anointing He would ever receive, and who better to do it than one who loved Him with earnest and undivided affection.

Mary's unparalleled act of sacrificial love so touched His heart that Jesus informed His disciples it would forever be proclaimed as a testimony of dedicated devotion and worship. He not only defended Mary that night, but He praised her and erected a towering monument to her. "I tell you the truth," He said, "wherever the gospel is preached throughout the world, what she has done will also be told in memory of her" (Mark 14:9).

Mary displayed a generous love that spared no expense, a passionate love that fell at His feet, a believing love that anointed her King for burial. Again, we never hear this woman of few words say anything in this incident. Her actions say it all, and history speaks for her. Indeed Mary's fragrant perfume has permeated the entire world.

## LESSONS FOR OUR OWN HEARTS

Wouldn't it be grand to have a heart like that of Mary of Bethany, fully affirmed by the Lord Jesus Christ? The great news for us is that it is possible, even probable, for those who become like her. But many will not believe this. "Why," they might ask, "put much effort into something unattainable?" They think some mediocre relationship with God as a friendly stranger is the best they can hope for in this life.

Oh, but they are wrong! This kind of relationship is not reserved for a special class of spiritual elites; God wants, even longs, for us all to have hearts filled with His treasure and to enter a life of wondrous intimacy with Him. That is a given. God's heart says yes to *you*. He pursues *you*. He lovingly created *you* to know Him. Believe it!

Still, as much as Christ longs for our fellowship, those who have little heart for knowing Him will receive scant spiritual treasure and enjoy little intimacy with Him. "You will seek me and find me when you seek me with all your heart."[7] He loves all of His children, but He has reserved a secret place, a tent of meeting, a Holy of Holies, for His closest friends. The psalmist knew this well, announcing, "You who *live* in the shelter of the Most High, who *abide* in the shadow of the Almighty, will say to the LORD, 'My refuge and my fortress; my God, in whom I trust'" (Psalm 91:1-2 NRSV).

The relationship Mary enjoyed with Jesus boiled down to one thing—an undivided heart of love for Him. Do you have this kind of heart? When you sense Him softly calling you to Himself, how do you respond—by sitting at His feet, hanging on His words, finding ways to delight Him? Have you cleared your heart of what robs you of your devotion to Him so that your chief passion is for His glory? Or do your own pursuits make Christ a sideshow act in your life rather than the main event?

As you are aware, our busy culture presents us with many things that clamor for our attention and affection. With so many concerns, interests, priorities, and passions, how can we hope to give Christ undivided devotion? Our hearts are pulled in so many directions! How can we possibly love the Lord with all our heart, soul, mind, and strength?

We can change, by God's grace. Are you ready? Let's follow Mary's lead as we explore ways to become more wholehearted in our devotion. Here are some considerations for us:

*Do you resist a close personal relationship with Jesus Christ?* So often we resist intimacy with God because we have unwittingly erected roadblocks. Perhaps it is unconfessed sin or fear. Perhaps we have a hard time believing that God could really want intimacy with us. After all, He is God, and knowing all about us, well, how could He possibly want us near Him? So we hide. But we will never get to know Him this way. We must stop hiding and honestly face ourselves—and Him. As we confess our sins and our fears and bring before Him our broken places, His grace brings healing and enables us to give Him our hearts.

*Do you believe Jesus loves you and wants your fellowship?* Believe right now that God loves and cares for you deeply and that He *wants* your fellowship. He is not some abstract or distant deity somewhere. No, God knows and loves you and has already called you to Himself. Mary knew Jesus welcomed her and even loved having her sit at His feet. As with her, He is inviting you into His presence.

This is the kind of God we love—one who does not build barricades around Himself but who wants to draw us near Him. A deeper realization of this truth will help rekindle your heart's devotion. Mary responded by becoming a woman with one primary ambition in life. It did not matter that Martha, the neighbors, the disciples, or anyone else might misunderstand her. In every recorded instance, we see in Mary a heart earnestly desirous to fully know, understand, love, and be filled with Jesus.

*Will you give your relationship with Christ first priority?* While many of us desire to have a heart and life like Mary's, we settle for less. We have the desire but not the devotion. We let other things get in the way. "Yes, Lord, I want more of You!" But then we opt for surfing the channels or the Net! Or we get entangled in "the tyranny of the urgent," as Charles Hummel puts it. After deciding to seek God, we become inundated by other demands clamoring for our attention. Despite similar "crying needs," Mary chose the part that gave the Lord most pleasure—"the better part."

*Will you know* Him, *not just facts about Him?* What if Mary had chosen to stay in the kitchen, hoping to overhear a snatch here or there from Jesus? She could have asked someone else to fill her in later, right? Sure. She easily could have heard about Him somewhere other than at His feet. But her devotion was very specifically to the *person* of Jesus Christ, not to facts *about Him.* She would accept nothing less than Jesus Himself, her true spiritual treasure. Her heart drove her to give Him top priority.

Likewise, our devotional life must consist of diligently pressing in to know Christ personally. What a cheerless, passionless religion it is that only takes time to learn facts about Christ. Those who only know *about* Him fall quickly in times of trouble. Thus we must cultivate and nurture our relationship with Him. For you, it may mean renouncing passivity and pushing aside distracting thieves that rob your undivided affection for God. It might take crying out to Him to change your heart and show you what He wants you to do to deepen your love-relationship with Him.

I no longer want just to hear about you, beloved Lord, through messengers. I no longer want to hear doctrines about you, nor to have my emotions stirred by people speaking of you. I yearn for your presence.

JOHN OF THE CROSS, 1500S

*Will you keep reaching for greater revelations of Him?* I can remember many years ago watching an episode of the television program *Little House on the Prairie*. It was so romantic! The blind girl, also named Mary, sensed her teacher's love for her. She loved him and longed to know him better. Finally one day she asked if she could "study" his face. He was happy to let her know him better. She tenderly reached out and with both hands ran her fingers over his face, studying its form, feeling every part, smiling as she recognized how wonderfully handsome he really was.

In so many ways we are like this blind girl, longing to see our Teacher, our Lover, our Best Friend. We see through a glass darkly, but then we will see face to face. Meanwhile, we say, "May I see You?" as we reach out our hands to study as best we can. He is all too happy to bend His face to us. We smile as we grope, catching glimpses of His wondrous beauty. Our hearts soar in the joy of deeper discoveries of His person.

---

*Let us know, let us press on to know the LORD. . . . For I desire steadfast love and not sacrifice, the knowledge of God rather than burnt offerings.*

HOSEA 6:3, 6 NRSV

---

Allow time for studying Jesus' face as Mary did. Beyond Bible study times, draw near to Him by praising Him for His love, worshiping Him for His majesty, meditating on His goodness, contemplating His character, reflecting on His blessings. Soon you will become aware of His nearness, your heart will fill with rich treasure, and you will crave still more.

*Will you resist distractions?* When Martha got distracted and tried to pull Mary into her frenzied state, Mary pushed Martha's "need" aside and continued to give her attention to Jesus. A heart like Mary's maintains its focus while everything around it clamors for attention—even sincere but misguided loved ones who also love Jesus.

The Lord not only called Mary's choice "the better part," but He went on to declare to Martha that "it will not be taken away from her." Don't we have a hard time with that? We wonder how Jesus could count our sitting idly by as more significant than our precious service. Most of us with a strong work ethic have a hard time cultivating our inner life. It looks like loafing; it seems impractical. Ah, but what could be more important, more practical?

In all fairness to Martha, I believe her loving acts of service were generally a credit to her. Her failure, however, was that she became so task-oriented she could not discern the moment and comply with the Holy Spirit's leading. While she was lost in her flurry, Mary was lost in Jesus.

*Will you refuse dissuasions?* This world promises us trouble and confusion. Sometimes our situation becomes desperate, and we feel God has let us down. How do we respond? Do we run to Him, cling to His feet, sobbing our hearts out, yet loving Him still? Despite her trauma, Mary could not stop loving Jesus when He let her brother die. Her undivided heart had nowhere else to run but to Jesus. Those who in a day of peace have learned to sit at Christ's feet will likewise find hope and comfort at His feet in their day of trial. Mary's heart held her steady in the dark in-between time preceding the miracle.

A strong relationship with Christ is not optional in these times—it is vital! Fail in this, and other things will continually manage to put a barrier between you and Him; your heart will become dull. Depleted in good treasure, you will drearily trudge along in your spiritual walk.

"Return, O my soul, to your rest," the psalmist cried. Take more time to sit at Jesus' feet, beholding Him, loving Him, adoring Him, hanging onto His life-giving words, seeking to know His heart more fully. Let His Spirit touch and fill you. Even now He beckons you to come away and be with Him, breathing Him in, receiving His life. Make this your way of life, and all your efforts will become divinely empowered.

*As a deer longs for flowing streams, so my soul longs for you, O God. My soul thirsts for God, for the living God. When shall I come and behold the face of God?*

PSALM 42:1-2

The fruit of an undivided heart is an abiding love relationship with Christ. You draw upon His life, and He becomes your life. You no longer feel a separation; you no longer strive to enter His presence; you no longer force your praises; you no longer hold back in guilt and fear; you no longer wrestle with God; you no longer wonder what you will do first thing in the morning and last thing at night. You live in an abiding state of peace, trust, communion, rest. You no longer live your own life and cry out for more of His—no! He has become your life, your heart's treasure. You say with Paul, "I no longer live, but Christ lives in me." You wonder how you could ever have treated this divine Lover of your soul as just another item to check off on your "To Do" list.

Because Mary took time to know the Lord well, she not only understood His heart for her, but she understood His personal need. In a prophetic act that showed how closely attuned she was to God's heart, she poured the precious contents of her alabaster bottle on Jesus' feet. She may not have fully appreciated the significance of her action. Most service and worship offered in pure devotion to Christ possesses a value and meaning beyond our own comprehension. But when the truth finally came home to Mary that hers was the only anointing her Lord ever received, what joy must have filled her heart!

What is your precious alabaster bottle, your treasure? Will you offer it for Jesus? Will you pour on Him your best, anointing Him as your heart's King? Radical love for Jesus sometimes leads us to do foolish, impractical things. It recognizes His preciousness—not what is in the bottle—and seizes opportunities to pour it out for Him. Are you ready? An undivided heart says, "Yes!" As the sweet fragrance of Mary's deed filled the whole house, ultimately permeating the world, let us also permeate our world with the fragrance of our love for Jesus Christ.

## Heart Check

1. As you examine your heart, do you see it as undivided in its devotion for Jesus Christ?

2. What to you constitutes spending quality time with Jesus Christ? Do you have a great desire to do this?

3. How can you better set priorities so that you will not neglect precious time spent with Him?

4. What is the most important principle you can apply to your life from Mary's example?

5. Compose a prayer to God in response to this chapter's lessons.

# 10

## *Lot's Wife*

### THE DIVIDED HEART

GENESIS 19:1-26; LUKE 17:32.

IN THE CLASSIC ALLEGORY OF the Christian life, *The Pilgrim's Progress*, we meet a man named Christian fleeing from the City of Destruction. Because God intends to destroy the city with fire from heaven, Christian becomes a pilgrim on his way to a better city—the Celestial City. In one incident he and his pilgrim friend Hopeful come to the pillar of Lot's wife. The sight leaves them humbled and awestruck, and they vow never to forget its lesson.

The Bible sums up the entire life of Lot's wife in a few words: "But Lot's wife looked back, and she became a pillar of salt" (Genesis 19:26), and in the New Testament: "Remember Lot's wife!" (Luke 17:32). But these few words stab the conscience and challenge the heart. For ages this woman has captured imaginations the world over. What is it about Lot's wife that leaves such an indelible imprint on history? A decision she made reflected the bent of her heart.

In Mary of Bethany we witnessed an undivided heart, one fully devoted to the Lord and filled with His spiritual treasure. Lot's wife, however, had a Divided Heart. It was cluttered with other treasure—things that prevented her from fleeing her own City of Destruction and embracing the life of a pilgrim. So serious was her heart impairment that she could not follow God's call. For this she paid dearly, losing her life in a day of judgment.

Geologists claim to have pinpointed the ruins of this judgment that occurred some 4,000 years ago. They believe that what remains of Sodom lies beneath the shallow southern extension of the Dead Sea between Israel and Jordan. Today tourists still flock to see this site. The terrain, however, hardly makes for the typical tourist attraction. It is desolate, with no visible life or beauty. A seeming sign from God of when humanity sank to its lowest level, the sea's surface is the lowest spot on earth—a quarter of a mile below sea level. Temperatures are nearly unbearable, and the air is oppressive with heavy odors of salt and sulfur. Even to this day all signs point to a past cataclysm. It takes no imagination to think that God cursed and condemned this area forever. Yet thousands of years ago, things were much different, as we will see.

The story of Lot's wife begins with Abram (later renamed Abraham) and Lot's father, Haran, who were brothers. Haran died while Lot was still young, leaving his grandfather Terah to raise him. Terah moved from Ur of the Chaldeans, taking Abram, Abram's wife, Sarai, and his grandson Lot with him. They settled in Haran where Terah died.[1]

When God told Abram to leave this land, along with his household, and go to a new one—the Promised Land—he took Lot with him. Accompanying his uncle Abram on his holy pilgrimage, Lot was no stranger to the covenant promises. They traveled together for some time in Canaan and Egypt.[2] We don't know at what point Lot was married, but in all likelihood his wife came into his life early. We know very little about her relationship with God except that as a close relative by marriage of faithful Abram and Sarai, she had notable examples of godliness. We can probably learn much about her by studying the life of her husband.

Lot and his family benefited from Abram's favored status in Egypt and acquired a taste for its luxuries. They, no doubt, loved it there. Both men prospered and became the chiefs of two allied clans. Eventually the groups became too large to live and travel together. Both had so many possessions that when they got to Bethel, the land could not support them together. This led to quarrels among their herdsmen.

One day, anticipating deepening conflicts, Abram approached

Lot with a most generous proposal. "Let's not have any quarreling between you and me, or between your herdsmen and mine, for we are brothers," he said. "Is not the whole land before you? Let's part company. If you go to the left, I'll go to the right; if you go to the right, I'll go to the left" (Genesis 13:8-9). Abram was letting Lot have the pick of the land although, as the older of the two, he had that right.

When Lot noticed the loveliness of the Jordan valley, how it was like a lovely well-watered garden, he thought, *This is God's country— just like Egypt.* Lot's wife must have concurred, wondering why Abram had given them such an advantage.

There were five cities in the region—Sodom, Gomorrah, Admah, Zeboiim, and Zoar, the most prominent of which was Sodom.[3] Archaeological evidence points to an advanced civilization in the area at this time. Apparently they were prosperous agricultural communities supported by efficient irrigation systems. The tremendous productivity sustained a very large population. Excavations of tombs indicate that perhaps more than a million people had been buried in them.

Lot immediately seized his opportunity, betraying his eagerness to secure the land's bounty without thought of the spiritual consequences of his choice. Do we see his wife disapproving? No, she likely urged him on. So while Abram lived in Canaan, Lot and his wife migrated down the valley toward trouble.

While the Bible calls Lot a righteous man,[4] he lacked the heart of a true pilgrim. He was wealthy, and his wife must have had her fill of living in tents on the outskirts of the city. We can well imagine her desire for a fine house in keeping with their wealth. As her husband had lusted for the best, we can visualize her also lusting for the best of everything—and Sodom had it to offer.

Soon after their move, war broke out among the region's kings. Sodom and its allies revolted against their Mesopotamian rulers. They defeated Sodom and seized everything of value there and in Gomorrah, along with all the food. They also carried off Lot and his clan, along with his possessions. When Abram heard of it, he led a company to pursue the plunderers and rescue his relatives. He routed their captors and recovered all the booty, including many people from Sodom. In gratitude Sodom's king offered Abram all the recovered possessions. Abram wisely refused the reward, however, keeping an oath not to benefit from Sodom. He did not want to give Sodom's king any future occasion to claim he had made Abram rich.[5]

If only Lot and his wife had had such hearts. Sodom's grateful king would want to treat Abram's relatives well, and they were happy to oblige him. Glad to trade their former life as wandering pilgrims and strangers for a settled life in this world, we see their hearts progressively becoming more entangled in Sodom and its worldly treasures. First they moved "near Sodom";[6] later they lived "in Sodom";[7] finally Lot sat "in the gateway"[8] of Sodom.

As attested by his seat in the gate—a place of authority and status—Lot had prospered in Sodom and became a leader. Not only did his wife enjoy the prestige of being wealthy, but now she was the wife of a prominent man in the community. Yes, Sodom was good to her.

Sodom, however, was also exceedingly wicked. The prophet Ezekiel writes, "Now this was the sin of your sister Sodom: She and her daughters were arrogant, overfed and unconcerned; they did not help the poor and needy" (Ezekiel 16:49). The prosperity of the region that so impressed Lot and his wife probably fueled its wickedness. With so much material comfort and abundant leisure time, the citizens of Sodom grew morally lax and increasingly gave themselves over to sin of every kind.

What a sad commentary we have here of Lot and his wife. This couple had participated in one of God's greatest calls on a human life; they had no doubt heard the awesome revelations given to Abram. Yet they felt right at home in the most wicked place on earth. In all fairness, the Bible says Lot never approved of Sodom's immoral ways.[9] And while he and his wife were prominent citizens, they could do little to influence the city toward righteousness. Still, just like any worldly Christians with divided hearts, they tried to enjoy the best of both worlds. They could know the Lord, be saved and on their way to heaven, and all the while enjoy every temporal blessing the world has to offer.

Lot's wife was well aware of Sodom's immorality and that it had been getting progressively worse. She had navigated through it, managing to maintain a comfortable life there. But just how long could she manage to balance a desire to know and please God while making her home in this wicked city? The day of reckoning would soon come.

One day God visited his friend, whom He now called Abraham, and confided that He was about to take action against Sodom and Gomorrah because of their great sin. But Abraham interceded for the cities, and the Lord promised not to destroy them if He could find even ten righteous people there.[10]

Meanwhile it was the end of an ordinary day in Sodom. The sun was setting, and Lot sat at the city gate as usual. People were going home for dinner. The square was peaceful. Later the city's business life would be put to sleep, and its night life would take over, drastically altering the city's face. Nothing atypical about that though—everything seemed perfectly normal.

This night, however, was anything but normal. Holy angels in human form entered Sodom to survey the situation and gather the righteous before doom descended on the city. They found no righteous persons outside Lot's family. As they entered the city gate at dusk, Lot hospitably greeted them and strongly urged them to stay with his family that night. He knew Sodom and wanted to shield these men from the vile abuse that unsuspecting visitors generally received there. Hurrying the men into his home, he probably recognized that they were at the very least men of God.

We do not see Lot's wife entertaining her guests. Lot is the one who prepared a fancy dinner and even baked them bread. This might suggest that she did not welcome the strangers into her house. Did she sense in her spirit that God had sent her guests and that their visit might mean a disruption or even a threat to her security in Sodom? Perhaps her divided heart recoiled.

The two angels were about to experience the seamy side of life in Sodom. Their visit suddenly shattered the fragile peace in which Lot's family had lived for far too long. All the men of the city, both young and old, came with one intent to Lot's door, demanding that he send the visitors out to them so they could rape them. The

"Sodomites" showed unbelievable depravity, shouting their intent shamelessly in the streets. Homosexual rape would have been bad enough, but had the desired victims been ordinary men, they would surely have murdered them.

Lot courageously tried to shield his guests by going out and shutting the door behind him. In the midst of this riotous situation, he risked his own life as he begged the men of Sodom not to do this "wicked thing." The fury of their lust could not be checked, however, and Lot began to panic. Sodom had warped his spiritual and moral perspective. In the face of this crisis, he vacillated in confusion and suggested a shocking compromise. In his desperation to shield his guests, he offered the men his two virgin daughters instead! While protecting guests at any cost was customary, his solution shows just how much Sodom's sin had impacted him.

Lot had thought he enjoyed favor in the city. Now he learned that the people had never really accepted him. He could not sway them at all in their present state of inflamed passion, and his value judgment against their intended behavior only enraged them. The mob, threatening him with violence, shouted, "Get out of our way! This fellow came here as an alien, and now he wants to play the judge! We'll treat you worse than them!"

The entire drama must have terrified Lot's wife. You would think this incident, which nearly cost the lives of her husband, her daughters, her guests, and perhaps her own, too, would be enough to make her exclaim, "That's it! I've had enough! I'm ready to leave this godforsaken place!" But even as she cried for God to save them, it seems she never considered the possibility that she would be leaving her city.

Yet the verdict was in. The angels opened the door, pulled Lot back inside to safety, and struck all the men outside with blindness as a foretaste of what would come the next morning. If Lot's wife had ever doubted that these men were powerful angels from God, she did so no longer. She heard them ask her husband, "Do you have anyone else . . . in the city who belongs to you? Get them out of here, because we are going to destroy this place. The outcry to the LORD against its people is so great that he has sent us to destroy it" (Genesis 19:12-13). She now knew they had the power to carry out their promise.

The New Testament calls Lot a righteous man who was tormented day after day by the filthy things he saw and heard in Sodom.[11] He must have heard of similar atrocities against innocent victims on a frequent basis. But it was never quite enough to get him and his family to leave Sodom. His wife very likely hindered him, being unwilling to hear of any radical decision to upset her comfortable life. So they stayed on, digging in their heels, closing their eyes and ears to the grotesque wickedness that screamed daily at them.

Now in desperation Lot ran to find the men to whom his two daughters were betrothed. He pleaded with them, "Hurry and get out of this place, because the LORD is about to destroy the city!" Thinking he was joking, they refused to take him seriously. How tragic that Lot had so little credibility in their eyes. This is the result when Christians seek to compromise with the world.

Lot's wife must have gone to bed that night hoping the visitors would wake up in a better mood and let bygones be bygones. Things would surely look better in the morning! The next morning while it was still dark, however, the angels awakened her husband with urgent voices. "Hurry!" they commanded. "Take your wife and your two daughters who are here, or you will be swept away when the city is punished."

According to the account in Genesis 19, Lot hesitated and probably the rest of the family with him. His wife must have looked around at her home, wondering if she had time to pack at least some of her things. But what would she leave behind? She loved it all! "Why," she muttered, "should I have to leave my home, my possessions, my friends, my standing in the community? Why, God? Why are You doing this to me? God, I know Sodom has its problems, but it will get better. This has been a good place for us. Think about it, God: We've prospered here; we like it here; we've built a life here. What about my husband's position, not to mention my daughters' pending marriages?" Part of her divided heart wanted to go God's way and escape His judgment, but another part loved her city.

Despite her reluctance to launch out, God extended a gift of grace to Lot's wife. She did not deserve it, but He sent His angels to her very doorstep to rescue her. They firmly grasped her by the hands and forcibly led her and her family out of the city. The Bible explains, "For the LORD was merciful to them." Indeed, what mercy! With what other mortals in the Bible did God's holy angels clasp hands?

As soon as they were outside the city limits, one angel made his command very clear: "Flee for your lives! Don't look back, and don't stop anywhere in the plain! Flee to the mountains or you will be swept away!"

Lot and his wife struggled with this new direction. They dragged their feet about leaving their sinful city behind. Still hoping to salvage something of their comfortable life in Sodom, they wanted a "city" of refuge instead of God's appointed mountain of refuge. Lot pleaded for a compromise, asking that the little city of Zoar be spared so they could go there instead. Showing immense mercy, an angel replied, "Very well, I will grant this request, too. . . . But flee there quickly, because I cannot do anything until you reach it."

Now that the angels no longer dragged Lot's wife by the hand, we can imagine her, with heart weighted down by worldly treasures, lagging behind the other three. She had not wanted to leave in the first place, and while she would much prefer moving to Zoar than to an uncertain life in the mountains, she grieved at leaving behind her home, relationships, and standing in the Sodomite community. Sad to say, when she arrived at Zoar, she was not thinking about God's mercy; she was mourning her losses.

Who would have thought that on such a bright, sunny, seemingly ordinary day, God would suddenly strike a disastrous blow? But as soon as the little foursome arrived in Zoar, the moment of reckoning descended upon the valley in a conflagration from heaven. The holocaust of destruction rained from the skies as fiery sulfur lashing and pummeling Sodom and Gomorrah. The furious thrashing turned the cities into smoking ruins, wiping them away forever.

God warned Lot's wife of the impending disaster. He tried to rescue her from His judgment. He even set her on the way to salvation, shepherding her to safety. But the bent of her heart was even more powerful than the grasp of angels leading her by the hand. She gave proof that she had never taken God seriously when she would not sever her heart-ties with Sodom. She came as close to deliverance without receiving it as was possible. Looking to the past, she destroyed her future. Having received the grace of God in vain,[12] she passed the point of no return. Not even the fire and brimstone falling around her could heal her divided heart.

Here we have the few Old Testament words that sum up this pitiful woman's life: "But Lot's wife looked back, and she became a pillar of salt" (Genesis 19:26). Her lingering, her longing, her looking back at the worldly delights of her home had crossed the line. The conflagration overtook her, the molten substance rained down on her, encrusting her in her salty tomb. She perished with her city.

In the region today a salt mass known as Gebel Usdum stands on the southwest shore of the Dead Sea. The Jewish historian Josephus (c. A.D. 37-100) claimed that the pillar actually continued standing until his day and that he saw it. Early church fathers Irenaeus and Tertullian also spoke of its existence in their times. Today there are many pillars of salt in the area, some of which the Arabs have called Lot's wife.

We also find large deposits of sulfur (brimstone) and asphalt (bitumen pits) in the area. Most researchers confirm that some type of sudden and devastating destruction took place. This once-bountiful valley remains a dead sea even today. Nothing lives in it. Even the smell is offensive. God designed the entire landscape as a standing reminder for all ages of His wrath against sin.

We might feel inclined to ask why Lot's wife paid such a price for her error. Oh, but she sinned grievously against the Lord. Not only did she lack the pioneering pilgrim spirit required of those who leave their former lives for a better city, but she was in love with the sinful world. She showed her reluctance to leave a place so wicked in God's sight that He must mark it for destruction. What she left behind and still held in her heart obviously was very dear to her, dearer than the treasures of God.

> *If they have escaped the corruption of the world by knowing our Lord*
> *and Savior Jesus Christ and are again entangled in it and overcome,*
> *they are worse off at the end than they were at the beginning. It would*
> *have been better for them not to have known the way of righteousness,*
> *than to have known it and then to turn their backs on the sacred com-*
> *mand that was passed on to them.*
>
> 2 PETER 2:20-21

Neglecting her heart is what cost this woman her life. Although she was struck dead on the spot, God did not let her body fall down, nor did it waste away. Instead it stood perpetually erect like a pillar, an enduring monument to the destruction that came to a person with a divided heart.

In the New Testament Jesus makes a short statement about this incident that He felt no need to clarify: "Remember Lot's wife." These words comprise one of the most powerfully convicting sermons ever preached.

## LESSONS FOR OUR OWN HEARTS

In this story we see two aspects of God's nature: His mercy and His wrath. We see mercy in that He would have spared the entire sinful city if He had found even ten righteous people in it. As it was, He rescued Lot's family. We see His wrath, however, as His fierce anger destroyed the city in one sweep of fiery indignation. Lot's wife, an object of mercy, was so close to salvation—only a turn of her head and heart away. She was almost saved, but that was not good enough.

How different was the outcome of Mary of Bethany with her undivided heart. While she stands out as a perpetual inspiration, Lot's wife stands as a perpetual warning. Scripture never names this tragic woman; we only know her by her all-too-evident divided heart. We can guess that she was right there behind her husband, just as we wives sometimes are, pushing him along in the direction of her own heart's choice. She should serve, as God intends, as a sobering warning to us all to guard ourselves against divided interests in our hearts.

From Lot's wife we see the ultimate consequence of a heart that holds two opposing treasures. But before that one final act that doomed her, she made many other mistakes along the way that confirmed there was something wrong in her heart. If she had seen the signs and taken them seriously, she could have checked her course. Perhaps she was not even aware of her heart's impairments. This lack of awareness, however, did not exempt her from disaster. So that we might discover any such impairments hiding in us, let's take a deeper look at these issues.

*When our heart is divided, we neglect God in our personal choices.* It takes singleness of heart to stay attentive to God's purpose for our lives. We see Lot's character in his early choice to take the best share of the land although it meant living near Sodom, a city known for its sin. We can see his wife right behind him, greedy and uncaring of the needs of Uncle Abram. They thought this was a wise choice, but it took into account only the needs of the flesh. They failed to realize that this choice would provide temptations powerful enough to destroy their family. After that first choice, their lives were a series of choices to compromise God's will.

We see Lot's soul vexed but never vexed enough to leave Sodom. He and his wife repeatedly seemed to choose what was expedient rather than the more difficult path of God's will. Isn't life a series of choices? We, too, can greedily choose to put ourselves first, disregarding the needs and rights of others, and most especially the Lord's will. But as we have seen, such choices lead to ever-increasing spiritual conflict in our hearts and lives. If we make our choices line up with God's direction by seeking His treasure first, we will never get sidetracked.

Have you chosen to live, work, and rub shoulders with those in a Sodom? Did you consult Him about this choice? Are you sure He sent you? If He did, glory to God—the church surely needs more missionaries. God commands us to reach those in the Sodoms of this world, but we must not let them reach us. If we become like them, we and our family may not recover from the damage done to our hearts.

But consider this: Don't we invite Sodom into our homes via the media on a daily basis? On any given night God's people often digest the same ungodly fare as everyone else. While Sodom's evil treasures continually get pumped into us, reading God's Word on any consistent basis seems like a real chore. When "something's on T.V.," God loses. The cracks in the divided hearts of multitudes of Christians keep widening as they choose soaps, sitcoms, and even Internet pornography over God's express command to flee the sinful city. Let us remember: The choice for God may seem difficult, but it is the one choice that is the right choice.

*When our heart is divided, we lose a godly witness.* Lot and his wife lived in Sodom so long and grew so complacent to the sins of their neighbors that their dull and tainted hearts provided no credible witness for God. They had no godly treasure to share even with their own family. Rather than influencing their environment, their environment shaped them. Like chameleons, they simply blended in with the crowd. Their compromise made them useless to God. When Lot finally did make a stand, who listened?

After his wife's death, Lot moved to the mountains with his daughters. Clearly, their shallow mother never raised them with the godly example they needed. They reflected more the morals of Sodom when, not trusting God to bring them mates, they conspired to get their father so drunk that he unknowingly impregnated them. Their mother's moral and spiritual witness to her family proved gravely deficient.

Evidence of their wickedness still remains: a continually smoking wasteland, plants bearing fruit that does not ripen, and a pillar of salt standing as a monument to an unbelieving soul. For because they passed wisdom by, they not only were hindered from recognizing the good, but also left for humankind a reminder of their folly, so that their failures could never go unnoticed.

WISDOM OF SOLOMON 10:7-8

(Note: The Wisdom of Solomon is in the Apocrypha. Although this literature is not Scripture, it contains some helpful insights, and this particular comment seemed especially appropriate here.)

If we would make a difference in our world, we must carefully maintain Christ as our heart's treasure. Then we can provide a godly witness to our family, our friends, and our world. We cannot afford simply to blend in with the environment. Dare to be different in your priorities, faith, and conduct. "You are the salt of the earth," Jesus says, "but if the salt loses its saltiness, how can it be made salty again? It is no longer good for anything, except to be thrown out and trampled by men" (Matthew 5:13).

We wonder why we don't see revival in our country. Isn't it because we have not yet cried out for a land where righteousness reigns? If we really wanted God to rule our land, we would want Him to rule our hearts and lives. As wholehearted, Spirit-filled Christians, we would make a profound impression upon our culture. But like Lot's wife, we are so absorbed in the culture around us that we have little godly influence and often even have an ungodly one.

*When our hearts are divided, we trust in worldly things for security.* Lot's wife had all that a woman of this world would want; she got everything she asked for. She built a weak moral and spiritual foundation and foresaw no time of testing that would make her life collapse. She was like the presumptuous ones who loaded onto the *Titanic*, certain it was unsinkable.

Worldly security is like that. Like a placebo that brings temporary relief to an incurable disease, such security fools us. Lot's wife looked back because she was more afraid of what lay ahead than behind. Sodom represented all that was stable, secure, nailed down in her life. Yet what true security can be found in a city—or a world—doomed to destruction?

We must abandon our attachments to this present world and embrace the values of God's kingdom. The people of the world will increasingly look for security in all the wrong places. But the Bible says, "No one finds security by wickedness, but the root of the righteous will never be moved" (Proverbs 12:3 NRSV). "When they say,

'There is peace and security,' then sudden destruction will come upon them . . . and there will be no escape!" (1 Thessalonians 5:3). Jesus followed His words, "Remember Lot's wife," with these: "Those who try to make their life secure will lose it, but those who lose their life will keep it" (Luke 17:33).

---

*You adulterous people, don't you know that friendship with the world is hatred toward God? Anyone who chooses to be a friend of the world becomes an enemy of God. . . . Come near to God and he will come near to you. Wash your hands, you sinners, and purify your hearts, you double-minded.*

JAMES 4:4, 8

---

*When our hearts are divided, we commit idolatry.* We may not bow down to a statue, but when our hearts elevate anything in our lives higher than God, we reveal our heart's true treasure. We must remove the things in our hearts that pull us away from Him. Jesus spoke of the "deceitfulness of riches."[13] Yet riches in themselves are not evil. Abraham was exceedingly wealthy, and his wealth never interfered with God's call. In sacrificing his own son Isaac, he proved that his heart had no idols. On the other hand, Jesus zeroed in on the Rich Young Ruler's idolatry when He told him, "There is still one thing lacking. Sell all that you own and distribute the money to the poor, and you will have treasure in heaven; then come, follow me" (Luke 18:22). Sad to say, the young man could not bring himself to make the break.

Lot's wife had likewise been unwilling to separate herself from the Canaanite world. Even knowing Sodom's deep wickedness did not stop her from wanting to be part of it. With its treasure entrenched in her heart, she had to be forced to go along when it was time to flee.

The first great commandment is to love the Lord with all your heart. You might ask yourself, "Are there things standing in the way of my loving God with *all* my heart? Are there things I refuse to give up for Him because I am unwilling to live without them?" Whatever you refuse to surrender to God is what you love most. A substitute for God, it makes you an idol worshiper.

Lot's wife's idolatrous desire for possessions, wealth, and prestige cost her everything. Likewise, a longing for prosperity can entice and enslave us if our hearts do not line up with God's will. While some people even make a sanctimonious religion of prosperity, Jesus urges us to "remember Lot's wife."

*When our hearts are divided, we hesitate at God's call.* Lot hesitated when the angel said to flee, and surely his wife did the same. Sodom had hypnotized them both. Before criticizing them, however, we should carefully observe our own hesitancy to obey God. How attracted are you by our culture's allurements? Has God called you to give up more than you are willing to surrender? Do you hold back, wistfully hoping somehow you won't have to give up the comforts of your home in this world? Believers must flee the world and avoid regretfully looking back with sad longing lest they be damaged or destroyed.

Don't begin to flee and then falter, or you will be like the hesitant person with one foot in the rowboat and the other on the shore. This is God's rowboat, and He has merely come to rescue you. Not about to let His boat be tied to Sodom's sinful shore, He begins to turn it back out to sea. You have no time for hesitation; you must make a quick choice. What will it be?

*When our hearts are divided, we look back to the world.*

---

*Another said, "I will follow you, Lord; but let me first say farewell to those at my home." Jesus said to him, "No one who puts a hand to the plow and looks back is fit for the kingdom of God."*

LUKE 9:61-62

---

Lot's wife shows the real peril of professing believers who seek to hang onto the things of the world. She had so adopted Sodom's values and was so unhappy with leaving, even after the horrid scene the previous night, that she lagged behind enough to get caught by the catastrophe. An expeditious flight from Sodom required releasing worldly interests, casting off worldly entanglements and liaisons. To the degree that she remained attached to Sodom, she could not flee to God in her heart. Clinging to the past, she turned back toward smoldering Sodom. God was not her refuge; Sodom was. He was not her treasure; Sodom was. She was out of Sodom, but Sodom was not out of her.

In like manner, we observe the Israelites beset with minor trials compared with the plagues they had escaped in Egypt, and yet they longingly looked back. "Let us choose a captain," they declared, "and go back to Egypt" (Numbers 14:4). Of this incident Stephen said, "Our ancestors were unwilling to obey him; instead, they pushed him aside, and *in their hearts they turned back to Egypt*" (Acts 7:39, emphasis added).

Do you look back longingly at your sinful past while trying to move forward into God's purposes? It will not work. You cannot flee forward while looking back. As long as you hold on to remnants of your old life, you can never make progress with God. The past will keep hanging you up as if you had a suspender caught on a nail. For, as Jesus explained, "No one can serve two masters" ( Matthew 6:24).

While Abraham *looked forward* to the city that has foundations, whose builder and maker is God,[14] Lot's wife looked toward the city without heavenly foundations, the earthly city of Sodom, choosing the pleasures of this present time over concerns for eternity.

*When our hearts are divided, we are not ready for Christ's return.*

---

*Likewise, just as it was in the days of Lot: they were eating and drinking, buying and selling, planting and building, but on the day that Lot left Sodom, it rained fire and sulfur from heaven and destroyed all of them—it will be like that on the day that the Son of Man is revealed. On that day, anyone on the housetop who has belongings in the house must not come down to take them away; and likewise anyone in the field must not turn back. Remember Lot's wife.*

LUKE 17:28-32

---

Why did Jesus tell us to remember Lot's wife? He gave these words in a teaching about His Second Coming. This makes the story of Lot's wife extremely relevant to us who live at the close of the age. Jesus directly applied this admonition to our own deliverance from the catastrophe that will overtake this godless world at His coming. He wants us to fix in our minds the tragic results of not being prepared for our departure. Only as we avoid the failure of Lot's wife, can we be ready for Christ's sudden return. When He comes, we will have no second chances.

Jesus suggests that the primary sin of Lot's wife was that she did not want to leave behind her house and possessions. Her *look back* proved her heart's desire to *go back*. Thus Jesus warns us against falling away from our faith. As believers, we have renounced the world and the sinful desires of the flesh. We have set our faces toward God's kingdom. Yes, we are still "pilgrimaging" our way through this world's plain en route to our final deliverance. If we return, however, to the things we have professed to have abandoned, it will be to our great loss.

Business was good, and the people were prosperous in Sodom and Gomorrah. They saw no indication that God would unleash His wrath that fatal day. Likewise, on the day Christ returns, people will not expect it. Even so, He will swoop down upon them like a thief in the night. He warns us to keep aware of the signs—looking up, not back.

When Jesus warns us to remember Lot's wife, He is saying some specific things: that when you barely escape with your life, you don't worry about what you leave behind; that giving up your possessions is preferable to trying to leave with them; that letting them perish is preferable to perishing with unbelievers; that holding the treasures of God's kingdom in our hearts should be our first concern. When God says, "Escape with your life; Save yourself from this crooked generation," we must make our escape and not look back. Turning back may have seemed like a minor infraction to Lot's wife. But it is all too evident that the sin of a divided heart was extremely serious.

> *For you need endurance, so that when you have done the will of God,*
> *you may receive what was promised. For yet "in a very little while, the*
> *one who is coming will come and will not delay; but my righteous one*
> *will live by faith. My soul takes no pleasure in anyone who shrinks*
> *back." But we are not among those who shrink back and so are lost,*
> *but among those who have faith and so are saved.*
>
> HEBREWS 10:36-39 NRSV

Oh, how we need to keep a pilgrim spirit about us. We are strangers and sojourners in this present world. Since having a divided heart is such a dangerous thing, we should ever strive to follow God wholeheartedly, not looking back but pressing forward toward our true City.

Do you have a personal Sodom? Is there something that this life holds for you that divides your heart? Don't let your heart cry, "I must have my Sodom!" On the contrary, if God is trying to send you away from it, then go forward, and don't even give a sideways glance back. If you *look back*, perhaps your heart has either already *gone back,* or it never really left. Don't leave your heart in Sodom.

Lot's wife was related to a righteous man; she was a better person than her neighbors; she heard the message of doom; God mercifully delivered her out; angels led her by the hand; she even made some effort toward obedience. Still, her divided heart ruined her in the end. Looking back to the place where she loved to live, she became a pillar of salt, a lasting monument of God's displeasure with those who turn back. Lot's wife received God's grace, but it was all for nothing. His Word entreats us, "We urge you also not to accept the grace of God in vain" (2 Corinthians 6:1 NRSV). "Note then the kindness and the severity of God: severity toward those who have fallen, but God's kindness toward you, provided you continue in his kindness; otherwise you also will be cut off" (Romans 11:22 NRSV).

When can you truly say that Jesus Christ is your treasure? When you leave your sinful past under the atoning blood of Christ; when you regret nothing you have left behind; when you love your Lord more than all else; when you embrace His call on your life—only then can you say your heart is no longer divided, that Jesus Christ has become your heart's treasure. You will look forward, and you will go forward with unflinching resolve; you will face your destiny with unshakable confidence; you will arrive at your destination with joy and victory. "For here we have no lasting city, but we are looking for the city that is to come" (Hebrews 13:14 NRSV).

## Heart Check

1. When your life is over, what perpetual memorial would you like to leave—the memorial of an undivided heart as with Mary of Bethany or the memorial of a divided heart as with Lot's wife?

2. Have you heard God's voice but not heeded His call in any areas of your life? How much of your security is tied to this present world? If God's Spirit says, "Flee Sodom and don't look back," is your heart prepared to go?

3. What steps can you take now to mend your heart and become single-hearted?

4. What is the most important principle you can apply to your life from the example of Lot's wife?

5. Compose a prayer to God in response to this chapter's lessons.

# 11

## *Abigail*

### THE PRUDENT HEART

1 SAMUEL 25:2-31; 27:3; 30:5; 2 SAMUEL 2:2; 3:3

THE SERVANT CAME TEARING breathlessly up to Abigail. "It's Nabal," he said. "He's gone and done it this time! We're all dead if you don't do something—and quick!"

"What did he do today?" she asked, standing to listen. She was used to fixing things for her troublesome husband. Whatever had happened, she was ready. From long years of experience, from a host of crises caused by him, she had learned the skills of conflict resolution.

Abigail was a God-centered woman who put Him first in all she said and did. The model of feminine grace and beauty, she was also a woman of admirable wisdom. Those around her had come to trust her judgment implicitly. If anyone could "pour oil on troubled water," she could.

Culturally, women of that time had little influence. This day, however, Abigail would boldly yet discreetly enter the domain of men and place herself between two powerful and intransigent egos—that of her wealthy husband who had acted like a fool and that of a mighty warrior who was about to act like one. Deliberately going out to meet a bloodthirsty army of 400 angry men, she would take control of an out-of-control situation. By quick thinking, decisive action, wise words, and a humble spirit she would single-handedly broker peace and save her household from carnage.

We call Abigail's heart The Prudent Heart. This heart knows the best course of action to take because it sees in advance the probable consequences of various options. Abigail's prudent heart let her exercise sound judgment with positive results.

---

*House and wealth are inherited from parents, but a prudent wife is from the LORD.*

PROVERBS 19:14 NRSV

---

The NIV Bible calls Abigail "an *intelligent* and beautiful woman."[1] A better rendering of the Hebrew word *sekel* would be "prudence." Yes, she had a high IQ, but as she studied history, the teachings of the prophets, and current events, she sought and gained spiritual insight. The good treasure poured into her heart made her a wise prognosticator.

However, Abigail bore enormous personal burdens. While her husband, Nabal, was descended from Israel's great hero Caleb, Nabal bore no resemblance to God's faithful servant. Abigail's husband was a mean-spirited, worldly boor. He was also a greedy, uncharitable ingrate who thumbed his nose at God and disdained those who served him. Evil in all his dealings, he was dishonest, oppressive, and lacked any sense of honor. Often he got obnoxiously drunk. Fittingly, his name means "obstinate fool."

Abigail, on the other hand, was one of the Bible's loveliest women. Their marriage was a complete mismatch. In fact, never were there two such opposites! We might ask why this virtuous woman married ill-tempered, foolish Nabal. In that time and culture, women had little say in whom they married. Since Nabal was rich (probably by inheritance), her parents thought he would be a good provider for their daughter. Her feelings were not uppermost in their minds as they secured one of the region's wealthiest men for her. Although Abigail's name meant "Father's joy," her father could not have seen joy in his daughter when he gave her in marriage to Nabal!

Even though Abigail was locked into a terribly difficult marriage with a wicked man, she matched his imprudence with her prudence. What he lacked in grace, she made up for. She had skills to make or break him, but she had character to make the noble choice. Deciding to "make the best of a bad bargain," she bore with his faults, doing all she could to preserve him. She never stooped to his level but kept her dignity and poise, doing what was best for him and his household.

Truly Abigail was a great woman, possibly the key to Nabal's success. Despite his follies, she stood gallantly with this man who did not deserve her, putting out his fires, acting as peacemaker between him and his neighbors, walking a tightrope of difficulties as she managed the household. While her marriage appears loveless and childless, her adversities produced diamonds in her character.

Abigail and Nabal lived in a city of Judah called Maon. Nabal also had property not far away in Carmel, Abigail's hometown.[2] He owned 1,000 goats and 3,000 sheep and had his sheep-shearing business in Carmel.

During this time God was shaking King Saul loose from his throne. The Lord had rejected Saul as king and chosen David, Israel's military hero, to succeed him. God had even led Samuel to anoint David as king. But Saul, bent on retaining the throne, sensed David's calling and relentlessly sought to destroy him. David and his small force of 600 men thus lived like outlaws, "moving from place to place."[3]

After Samuel died, David made the desert east of Maon his hiding place. The area had no police force, and wandering bands of marauders as well as natural predators posed a terrible threat to flocks, herds, and shepherds. Encamped near Nabal's large flocks, David and his men had voluntarily patrolled the area, doing everything in their power to help the shepherds. Nabal had no doubt heard about this valuable service.

It was sheep-shearing season, and Nabal had brought his flocks in from pasture and was shearing them. A festival time in Israel, sheep owners celebrated and showed their gratitude to God, their workers, and their neighbors by providing a large feast. They customarily also shared their bounty with the poor and needy. Many guests had gathered at Nabal's property for his feast, and David got wind of it. Since goodwill was in the air, he thought this an opportune time to remind Nabal of his faithful protection that year and ask for some food. He had every reason to believe Nabal would want to share generously with him and his hungry men.

So David called ten young men and said, "Go up to Nabal at Carmel and greet him in my name. Say to him: 'Long life to you! Good health to you and your household! And good health to all that is yours! Now I hear that it is sheep-shearing time. When your shepherds were with us, we did not mistreat them, and the whole time they were at Carmel nothing of theirs was missing. Ask your own servants and they will tell you. Therefore be favorable toward my young men, since we come at a festive time. Please give your servants and your son David whatever you can find for them'" (1 Samuel 25:5-8).

This was a very polite request. It shows high regard for Nabal, blessing him, his household, and all that he owns. Giving Nabal the humble respect of a son to his father, David calls himself "your son David." It appeals to Nabal to recognize the character of David and his men, that despite their own scarcity, they took great care to protect Nabal's flocks. It even enlists the testimony of Nabal's own shepherds to verify the story. Demanding nothing, it simply asks for a modest "whatever."

So with utmost courtesy and respect, the men delivered their humble request. Since those who show kindness can normally expect to receive kindness, they were certain of returning to David loaded down with provisions. But, fool that he was, Nabal lived up to his name and responded cavalierly, "Who is this David? Who is this son of Jesse? . . . Why should I take my bread and water, and the meat I have slaughtered for my shearers, and give it to men coming from who knows where?"

The men felt the insult deeply. Custom demanded that Nabal repay their kindness. Yet the arrogant landowner treated David as an insignificant rebel whom he could disregard. Nabal's act was inexcusable. Rather than respond to his rude and provocative behavior, David's men said nothing and left.

Nabal must have thought that he was a truly great and powerful man as his workers sheared his thousands of sheep. It had been a good year. Ka-chink! Ka-chink! Ka-chink! He could just hear the money flowing into his coffers. He got so full of himself that he thought no one could touch him—not even the powerful military man David. What a fool!

The men told David every word of Nabal's rude rejection. Completely taken off guard, David was furious! Quite out of character, he decided to get revenge: He would plunder Nabal's goods, killing him and every male in his household. Nabal had rendered evil for good, and now David would render evil for evil. Summoning his men, he shouted, "Put on your swords!"

A servant of Nabal's who had witnessed the incident ran to Abigail. If anyone would know what to do, she would. She saw the fear in his face as he explained their indebtedness to David and his men. "They did not mistreat us, and the whole time we were out in the fields near them nothing was missing. Night and day they were a wall around us all the time we were herding our sheep near them." Then he said, "Now think it over and see what you can do, because disaster is hanging over our master and his whole household. He is such a wicked man that no one can talk to him" (1 Samuel 25:10-17).

Abigail must have wondered how her husband could be so stupid. How could he rudely deny those who had come in peace to ask only that to which they were entitled? Didn't he know David could destroy their home and family with one swipe? Didn't he recall that crowds had sung of the famed young warrior, "Saul has slain his thousands, and David his tens of thousands" (1 Samuel 18:7)? Nabal had gone beyond the pale, David would be justly offended, and the servant was right—she had to do something.

It is a tribute to Abigail that the servant, fearing for his life, turned to her. She had intervened for her husband in ugly altercations before. Her prudence had won the servant's utmost respect and loyalty. He believed in her ability to solve the worst of problems.

From years of experience, Abigail knew that trying to reason with Nabal would do no good. Contrary to the customs of the time, she took the initiative and went around him, risking his anger, realizing the greater risk of doing nothing. She would not act impulsively, but God had invested rich stores of wisdom in her prudent heart.

Jesus told of one king's dealings with the king of a large advancing army: He would "send a delegation while the other is still a long way off and will ask for terms of peace" (Luke 14:32). This was Abigail's strategy—to intercept David and his men and negotiate peace with them before they got to Nabal.

With divine wisdom, she moved deftly to gather resources. She prepared a quantity of food large enough to satisfy David's immediate need. "She took two hundred loaves of bread, two skins of wine, five dressed sheep, five seahs of roasted grain, a hundred cakes of raisins and two hundred cakes of pressed figs, and loaded them on donkeys" (1 Samuel 25:18). David would have been thankful with much less from Nabal.

As Abigail came riding her little donkey into a shadowy mountain ravine, she spotted David and 400 of his men descending toward her. As they marched closer, she could sense their anger. But she had learned to keep her head under stress. Her heart kept her steady, and she felt confident of God's leading.

David had just told his men, "It's been useless—all my watching over this fellow's property in the desert so that nothing of his was missing. He has paid me back evil for good." Then he angrily vowed, "May God deal with David, be it ever so severely, if by morning I leave alive one male of all who belong to him!" Evidently not one of his men encouraged him to keep his head and not take Nabal seriously. They all wanted blood.

So when Abigail met them on the march, David was in no mood for mercy. But then again rarely had he met a woman like Abigail—beautiful, wise, persuasive, full of courage. Her strategy may seem well thought out, but she did not have time to contrive some brilliant scheme. What she did and said were simply the fruits of her prudent heart. Listen to her tactful approach as she mediates peace: "When Abigail saw David, she quickly got off her donkey and bowed down before David with her face to the ground." Displaying humility goes far in pacifying anger. This was not a false pretense; she did not manipulate but genuinely paid homage.

Now that she had David's ear, she began her persuasive speech, one of the longest by a woman in the Bible. In stark contrast to her husband who said, "Who is David?" she respectfully called him "my lord" and herself "your servant." She then begged him for a hearing: "My lord," she said, "let the blame be on me alone. Please let your servant speak to you; hear what your servant has to say." Through her gracious and obliging approach, she had already defused much of David's anger.

Then, pleading for mercy, she said, "May my lord pay no attention to that wicked man Nabal. He is just like his name—his name is Fool, and folly goes with him. But as for me, your servant, I did not see the men my master sent." In other words, David should not take Nabal's words personally, for the man was simply living up to his name. She pleads her own ignorance of the incident, suggesting that though Nabal is a fool, he is not so much one that he does not take her advice. If David's men had come to her, this unfortunate thing would never have happened.

Abigail's sweet voice of reason quelled David's tempest. Encouraging the best in him, she reinforced his desire to do the right thing. "Now," she said, "since the LORD has kept you, my master, from bloodshed and from avenging yourself with your own hands, as surely as the LORD lives and as you live, may your enemies and all who intend to harm my master be like Nabal."

Clearly, Abigail is not only on a mission to save lives in her household but to save God's plan for David's future. Avenging himself on Nabal and his innocent servants would tarnish David's character and his future reputation as God's anointed king. She wanted to prevent him from the bloodguilt he would always regret.

We see here the depth of Abigail's reverence for God. God, in His sovereign will, had called David and led him safely to this point. He was now intervening through Abigail in this present crisis to keep David in His plan. What an incredible insight from a woman who might have grown bitter at God in the harsh, unbending realities of her own life with Nabal.

Next Abigail pointed to her provisions, saying, "And let this gift, which your servant has brought to my master, be given to the men who follow you." Then she pleaded, "Please forgive your servant's offense, for the LORD will certainly make a lasting dynasty for my master, because he fights the LORD's battles. Let no wrongdoing be found in you as long as you live."

Seeing beyond the present circumstances to when David will no longer be a fugitive and outlaw but the king of all Israel, she pointed David back to God, appealing to that higher purpose. David is God's servant whom God would raise up for his faithfulness to fight the Lord's battles, not his own. Hence, the Lord would care for David and fight his personal battles for him. No enemy could withstand God's plan.

Abigail did not name Saul, but she knew Saul was seeking David's life. She went on to speak prophetically: "Even though someone is pursuing you to take your life, the life of my master will be bound securely in the bundle of the living by the LORD your God. But the lives of your enemies He will hurl away as from the pocket of a sling." Her metaphor denotes God's watchful care over David's life, assuring him that his troubles will soon blow over, that God will take care of him, and that he should wait for God's vindication.

Still prophesying, Abigail closed her argument, saying, "When the LORD has done for my master every good thing he promised concerning him and has appointed him leader over Israel, my master will not have on his conscience the staggering burden of needless bloodshed or of having avenged himself." What an encouraging affirmation after such a discouraging incident. Surely David wanted no "staggering burden" of sweet-revenge-turned-bitter tarnishing his glorious future. To forgive Nabal would spare him from having a regrettable bloodstain on his name. Abigail ended her plea with one final petition: "And when the Lord has brought my master success, remember your servant" (1 Samuel 25:21-31).

A prudent heart never resorts to manipulation, and Abigail never flattered David. She sincerely spoke what she knew to be true, and this by revelation of God. Not only did she have wise and persuasive words, but she backed up her respect for David by giving him the provisions Nabal had denied him.

Abigail's words left David dumbfounded and conscience-stricken. How clouded his vision had been! How full of hatred his heart had become! He probably remembered his own maxim: "Let the righteous strike me; let the faithful correct me" (Psalm 141:5 NRSV). He humbly and gratefully received her correction. She had literally come between him and the awful sin he was about to commit.

With laments suddenly turned to praises, he exclaimed, "Praise be to the LORD, the God of Israel, who has sent you today to meet me. May you be blessed for your good judgment and for keeping me from bloodshed this day and from avenging myself with my own hands." Shaken, too, by thoughts of this lovely woman's near personal loss, he added, "Otherwise, as surely as the LORD, the God of Israel, lives, who has kept me from harming you, if you had not come quickly to meet me, not one male belonging to Nabal would have been left alive by daybreak."

David accepted Abigail's gift. "Go home in peace," he said. "I have heard your words and granted your request" (1 Samuel 25:32-35). As Abigail, her attendants, and her donkeys wended their way back through the pass, David's heart must have raced with gratitude and amazement. Just as he had subdued Saul's demons with his sweetly anointed harp-playing, Abigail with her own sweet tones had exorcized his vengeful demon of hatred and murder. She had saved not only her own household but the integrity of Israel's future king whom God had deemed the "man after his own heart."[4] David would remain untarnished to fulfill God's purposes in a God-honoring way.

This was a day of celebration and feasting after all. As David and his men joyfully broke into their provisions, perhaps he shook his head and said, "What a woman! That fool Nabal has no idea what he's got."

Abigail then returned to her role as dutiful advocate and protector of her miserable husband. When she got home, she saw that he "was in the house holding a banquet like that of a king."[5] Intoxicated, he was boisterous and full of himself, bragging to his guests, lavishly entertaining them. He had no idea he had very nearly brought disaster on his entire household that day; nor did he know how deeply he had offended God.

Abigail knew that if she told Nabal then what had occurred, he would be implacable. So she waited until the next morning when he was sober. Knowing her honest admission would be risky, that he might lose his temper, she still told him everything, sparing him no detail. She had taken Nabal for better or worse, and most of it had been worse, but her days of hard service were about to end. Instead of leaping to his feet in anger, Nabal suddenly slumped to the floor, suffering an apparent heart attack. About ten days later "the LORD struck Nabal and he died."[6]

Abigail would have no regrets as to her own faithfulness as a wife. She had stood with Nabal, and now she was legally free of her troubled marriage. She had never disgraced her husband or her wedding vows but had prudently navigated through her difficult commitment.

When David heard of Nabal's death, he felt doubly blessed. First Nabal had died a natural death and not by David's hand. God had fulfilled Abigail's words, thus proving he could always trust God for vindication. This was a principle David would live by for his entire career.

Second Nabal's death warmed the cockles of David's heart because he could not forget Abigail's petition to remember her. In fact, he could not get the lovely woman out of his mind! He was indebted to her and realized that her behavior more befit a future queen than his a future king. If she had managed to be such a good wife to a wicked man, she would surely be a great wife to a good man. Now that she was free to choose a good man, he wondered, *Why not me?*

So he sent his servants back to her farm with a proposal of marriage. The widow was no longer the one entreating but the one entreated. Still, with her characteristic self-abasement, she fell down before the men and replied, "Here is your maidservant, ready to serve you and wash the feet of my master's servants" (1 Samuel 25:41).

Abigail accepted David's proposal despite his present state as an impoverished fugitive living in caves and rugged mountain outposts. She would take on this life of hardship and danger because she believed in David's calling and that she could help him in it. She would go in faith, assured that God would fulfill His promises.

Quickly calling her five maids together, they left with David's men to begin a new life.

A suitable companion for Israel's future and great king, Abigail became David's wife. Little is said of her after this, but no doubt there were many more demands on her prudent heart. Hers was not an easy life, living with the band of outcasts, constantly avoiding enemies. When they moved into Philistine territory to escape Saul, the Amalekites carried off Abigail, among others. Fortunately David rescued them.

Theirs would be no perfect storybook marriage. Abigail was David's third wife, with more to come. While Saul had given David's first wife, Michal, to another, David also took a wife named Ahinoam. God had forbidden Israel's king from taking many wives; yet David chose to follow the practice of other royal courts in pagan countries and even of some of the patriarchs.

Still, Abigail was the wife best suited for David. They both were deeply devoted to God, and while "prudence" describes her, David was also known as a man "prudent in speech."[7] With her godly wisdom and counsel, she was a great asset to him. She inspired confidence in him and appealed to his highest nature. She knew that the future belonged to David. While Abigail remained childless with Nabal, she gave David his second son, Chileab, also called Daniel.

Though beautiful, Abigail did not use sensuality to manipulate men. Instead relying on the good treasure of her heart, she worked for their good. A prophetess, she saw the big picture of God's plan for David when he had lost sight of it. She advised him effectively, exercising diligent stewardship of the gifts God had given her. Her influence over this great man proved her own greatness. Swiftly and effectively, warmly and winsomely, she brought out the best in him.

Even representing a fool, Abigail had negotiated peace. While she never influenced Nabal deeply because he was a fool, she maintained personal virtue in her unhappy marriage. She stayed loyal but not blindly loyal. Despite her problem-ridden life, she acted prudently for him, her household, her future king, and her God. She was a godly woman, a good wife, and a wise diplomat.

## LESSONS FOR OUR OWN HEART

Prudence. Years ago this was a popular female name and a respected virtue. While it is not a popular name today, we should definitely recover it as a notable virtue, placing it high on our list of admirable character qualities.

A prudent heart comes from God, just as "Every good and perfect gift is from above . . ." (James 1:17). Still, this virtue, like others, must be developed. While many women focus on outward beauty, God wants us to make high priority of cultivating our hearts. If we would have prudent hearts, we must value this virtue, desire it, pray for it, and practice it. We must rid our hearts of what is worthless and let His Spirit deposit in us His good treasure.

---

*Prudence will watch over you . . .*

PROVERBS 2:11 NRSV

*Keep sound wisdom and prudence . . .*

PROVERBS 3:21 NRSV

*O simple ones, learn prudence . . .*

PROVERBS 8:5 NRSV

*I, wisdom, live with prudence . . .*

PROVERBS 8:12 NRSV

---

Prudent behavior did not come cheaply in Abigail's life. It was no doubt perfected through many heart-rending situations in her home. Her diplomatic and persuasive skills came through dealing with Nabal and with the scores of people he had offended. God has a wonderful way of using our trials to train us. Abigail's wellspring of spiritual purpose enabled her to grow in prudence through her miserable circumstances.

Some may see in Abigail a lack of submission to her husband Nabal. She did the exact opposite of Nabal's wishes. Not only did she feed David and his men, but she did it behind her husband's back!

Abigail, however, clearly demonstrated a submissive heart by simply staying married to such a fool. Her highest loyalty and submission was to God, as is ours. And love for her husband, fool though he was, motivated her to move contrary to his wishes.

A Christian wife's responsibility to submit ends when lives are jeopardized or when God's clearly revealed will is violated. She should never partner in sin, no matter who demands it. Abigail not only did what was best, but she should be praised for what she did. David did not think, *What a scheming, rebellious woman!* No, he commended her sound judgment, praising the Lord for sending her to avert bloodshed. The first person's life she saved was Nabal's! If one marriage partner endangers the family, the other has rights and responsibilities, too.

Sometimes we do not like to take initiative. Often Christian women abdicate their roles by unduly catering to husbands or children. They stay home from church to make peace with unbelieving husbands; they support wayward children by letting the children manipulate them. Lacking prudent hearts, they fail to seek the Lord's solution to their dilemmas and shrink from faith and obedience.

A woman I know well named Victoria had—yes, "had"—a difficult, unbelieving husband. Through the years she loved, served, and honored him in ways that I would have found extremely hard to do. While she died a thousand deaths to self, she never compromised her loyalty to Christ. Learning the lessons of a prudent heart, she was forthright with the truth but not argumentative. She prayed for him, showed him Christ's love, and forgave him. Eventually her prayers were answered. Her husband came to Christ. He adored her, cherished the good treasure in her heart, and, through the years, became softer and gentler. Now in their old age, they have a very enviable life together.

---

*Who then is the faithful and prudent manager . . . ? Blessed is that slave whom his master will find at work when he arrives. Truly I tell you, he will put that one in charge of all his possessions.*

LUKE 12:42, 44 NRSV

---

Abigail proved that one need not have a prestigious position to play a significant role in this world, that a prudent heart can open amazing doors and reap mighty results. Here are some things in Abigail to emulate:

She was not ignorant of national affairs, including issues between her king and the future king. Her knowledge contributed to her effectiveness.

Neither shrinking in self-protection nor presumptuously running out with sword and banner flying, she found the best solution for everyone.

She responded to God's wisdom by acting quickly and decisively.

She cooled David's temper by "pouring oil on troubled water" with gentle words and a gracious deed.

She saw the big picture and used that vision to encourage David.

Rather than becoming angry and bitter over her troubling husband, she committed her life to God. Thus she could advise David to leave his vindication to God's justice.

Just as Satan used Nabal to assault David emotionally, making him forget who he was in God's eyes, Satan assaults us. It takes one with a prudent heart to help languishing souls regain their perspective. Once renewed in hope, they see that all is not for nothing. They are still God's children, His plans for them are not over. Do you have people like this in your life? Do you try to be this type of person?

In our day Christians in many places are extremely hard pressed. How should they respond when Muslim, Hindu, or other extremists burn down their churches or threaten their homes and loved ones? Should they retaliate? Should they lie down in the street and be run over? These are perplexing questions for which there are no easy answers. It takes prudent hearts to lovingly "heap burning coals" on our enemies' heads and to "not be overcome by evil, but overcome evil with good."[8]

We see in Abigail's story the two kinds of wisdom (and two kinds of heart treasure) to which James refers—the "earthly, unspiritual, devilish," and the kind that guided Abigail, a wisdom that is "first pure, then peaceable, gentle, willing to yield, full of mercy and good fruits . . ." (James 3:15, 17). The world desperately needs today's Abigails to step forward and overcome the damage inflicted by oppressive Nabals and vindictive Davids.

There are other lessons for us in this story. First, as an old proverb says, "Marry in haste, repent at leisure." If we marry without proper consideration, we may have a lifetime to regret our choice. Second we should beware of being "unequally yoked"[9] with an unbeliever. We cannot plan to marry a Nabal and change him. Today women have great freedom, but many lack the prudent hearts to guide them wisely into God's design for their lives.

God will graciously work in our mistakes for ultimate good as we learn to trust Him by making the best of our situations. Many noble women, like Abigail, have fools for husbands but "turn their lemons into lemonade." By their prudent hearts, their husbands are "won over without a word by their wives' conduct."[10] If you have a difficult man, not only can you learn to live with him, but you can make the best of your marriage. With good treasure in your heart, God can still use you powerfully to bless your home, your community, your church, and even your world.

### Heart Check

1. Do you have a prudent heart? Can you think of times when God has used your prudence?

2. Has someone ever treated you unfairly? How did you respond? How can you respond more prudently next time?

3. Read Proverbs 31. How does the quality of prudence relate to this woman? How does she compare with Abigail?

4. What is the most important principle you can apply to your life from Abigail's example?

5. Compose a prayer to God in response to this chapter's lessons.

# 12

## *Delilah*

### THE MANIPULATIVE HEART

#### JUDGES 16:4-22

BEAUTIFUL, SEDUCTIVE, POTENTLY sensual, irresistibly feminine—her name was Delilah. Her name in Hebrew can be translated "feeble," but there was nothing feeble about her. She was
indefatigably spirited, devilishly shrewd, mentally agile, and posi-
tively charming. Her name can also be translated "devotee," which
suits her better, since she devoted herself to her all-consuming
goal—to get rich.

Despite her external loveliness, Delilah had the cold, con-
scienceless heart of a beast. Given to evil and deceit, devoid of God's
treasure, she would reach her goal by ruining the man who loved her,
even while feigning love for him. Love and loyalty were foreign con-
cepts to her. Doing whatever it took, even plotting her lover's demise,
she lustily seized her prize.

We call her heart The Manipulative Heart. While we saw a prudent heart in Abigail that enabled her to bring life and blessing to the
men in her life, Delilah's heart led her to manipulate her man for selfish gain. Taking advantage of his infatuation with her, she deluded
him into believing she loved him and that he could trust her with his
most closely guarded secret. Interestingly, the Arabic translation of
the name Delilah is "flirt." Whatever the truest meaning of her name,
she represents all who use their seductive charms to manipulate others for selfish ends. Having tarnished the name Delilah forever, it has
become a synonym for a seductive woman.

*For these commands are a lamp . . . keeping you from the immoral woman. . . . Do not . . . let her captivate you with her eyes, for . . . the adulteress preys upon your very life.*

PROVERBS 6:23-26

Samson and Delilah's story is the tale of an unfortunate man with a weakness for women and the woman who captured his eye, snared his heart, shipwrecked his ministry, and made mincemeat of his life. Samson was a great man, but Delilah single-handedly influenced him to betray his unique calling from God, thereby preventing him from reaching the full potential of his greatness.

Their story takes place during the time before Israel had kings, when "the Lord raised up judges"[1] to lead the nation and rescue it from enemies. It was a cyclical era during which Israel went from defeat to victory to defeat again, depending upon the nation's allegiance to the Lord. At one point, when the Lord delivered the sinful nation into Philistine hands for forty years, an angel visited an Israeli woman. He promised her a son who would be a Nazirite[2] from birth to death and begin Israel's deliverance from the Philistines. When the baby was born, his mother named him Samson. "He grew and the LORD blessed him" (Judges 13:24).

Against his parents' wishes, Samson married a Philistine woman. The Lord prompted his action, however, to set the stage for ending Philistine rule. At his wedding feast, Samson gave his Philistine guests a wager. If they solved his riddle, he would pay them; but if they could not, they must pay him. Unable to come up with the answer, they went to Samson's bride and threatened her into coaxing the solution from him. If she failed, they swore to kill her and her entire family.

She went to work, and she worked hard! She threw herself on him sobbing, "You hate me! You don't really love me. You've given my people a riddle, but you haven't told me the answer." The feast lasted seven days, during which she pestered him relentlessly. Finally he gave in and told her the riddle, providing us the first clue to his vulnerability to feminine charms.

After his wife told the Philistines the riddle's solution, they gave it to Samson. He exploded in anger: "If you had not plowed with my heifer, you would not have solved my riddle!" (Judges 14:16-18). This initiated a chain of events that ended in the poor woman's death at Philistine hands.

After this, Samson and the Philistines became mortal enemies. Whenever God's Spirit came upon him, he received supernatural strength and conquered his Philistine adversaries. In one exchange, Samson took a donkey's jawbone and struck down 1,000 Philistines who had attacked him. Following this victory Samson became Israel's judge. Through his twenty-year tenure, the Philistines' grip on Israel progressively weakened.

Once, when Samson went into Philistine territory, he got waylaid by a prostitute. When the Philistines heard where he was, they plotted to kill him at dawn. But Samson left in the night. Finding the city gate locked tight, he tore loose its massive doors, along with their posts, and carried them off on his shoulders.[3]

The Philistine rulers came to realize they could never match Samson's physical strength. Thinking he must have some special secret charm or magic spell related to his phenomenal strength, they decided to find a way to get at it.

It so happened that Samson had fallen in love again, this time with an irresistible woman named Delilah who lived in the valley of Sorek, not far from his hometown. The Philistines got wind of it. Knowing his weakness for the seductive charms of women, they thought they might have found the exploitable grain of softness in the man of granite strength.

Since "plowing with his heifer" had worked before, they decided to approach Delilah. They probably knew of her beauty and her skill at handling the opposite sex. Her sexual morals may have been a match to Samson's, and perhaps others before him had regularly spent the night with her. They hoped a woman like Delilah would quickly accept their plan, *if* the price was right.

At the time five rulers governed the Philistines, each living in a different prominent city: Ashdod, Ashkelon, Ekron, Gath, and Gaza.

Forming a coalition, these five rulers converged on Delilah's house. They made an impressive delegation as they knocked at her door. This was top-secret, high-level stuff, and Delilah was all ears. The rulers explained their failure to subdue Samson and their hope for her help. Coaxing her, they said, "See if you can *lure* him into showing you the secret of his great strength and how we can overpower him so we may tie him up and subdue him" (Judges 16:5).

Think about that word *lure*. Whether used as a noun or verb, it includes the use of wiles or temptation to attract a victim. The actual Hebrew word used here, *pathah*, means to entice, deceive, flatter, or allure. These powerful men knew this task best suited a woman. Delilah agreed but wondered what was in it for her. The men answered before she could ask: "Each one of us will give you eleven hundred shekels of silver."[4] Wow—5,500 pieces of sterling was no small amount! In the Bible's next chapter, a young Levite accepts payment of room and board plus ten shekels a year for his services.[5]

They had pushed the right button—greed! Delilah's eyes glistened. Won to their cause, she would lock onto her goal with the determination of a fire ant. Yes, she would conquer the unconquerable man. It would be easy. After all, she already owned his heart. Captive to her charms, he was putty in her hands! She had no qualms at all about betraying him.

We do not know whether Delilah was a Jew or a Philistine. In that the Philistines did not appeal to their common national loyalty, she may have been an Israelite. If she were a Jew, her betrayal would not only destroy Samson but would damage her own people and nation since she would ruin their judge, champion, and defender. In any case, she proved she had the heart of a Philistine.

While previously one woman by her feminine devices had wrested a riddle's secret from Samson, the stakes had dramatically increased in this new situation. The secret Delilah would go after was one he had never divulged in his whole life, one that could mean the difference between life and death for him and between victory and defeat for his people. Would he now betray it to a woman he loved? Like a black widow spider, Delilah began to spin her web of sexual enticement and manipulation. If anyone could succeed in bringing down this man, she could.

Of course, Samson was not without sin in the matter. Uncontrolled lust blinded him to God's leading in his life, and he was in sinful sexual bondage to his paramour. The years of service to Israel had been long and wearying. He may have thought Delilah provided the chance for the happiness he had always wanted. Spending increasing time at her house, he found it a sanctuary of delight. She had become his preoccupation, and he was about to become hers.

---

*An enemy dissembles in speaking while harboring deceit within; when an enemy speaks graciously, do not believe it, for there are seven abominations concealed within.*

PROVERBS 26:24-25 NRSV

---

Delilah slithered toward her target like a snake in the grass. At the first opportune moment, when Samson felt especially satisfied with her love, the temptress mischievously began her campaign. First sweetly staring at his rippling muscles in a wide-eyed wonder bound to flatter him, she said, "Tell me the secret of your great strength and how you can be tied up and subdued" (Judges 16:6).

He had been down this road before and had no intention of telling her. But he loved matching wits, using riddles and mental games, so he hoped to turn off her curiosity with some playful banter. He replied, "If anyone ties me with seven fresh thongs that have not been dried, I'll become as weak as any other man."

Delilah, already mentally stuffing her moneybags, excitedly sneaked off to tell the Philistines the news. They sent her back with seven fresh thongs and some soldiers whom she sequestered in an adjoining room. When Samson was asleep, she tied him up with the thongs and hollered, "Samson, the Philistines are upon you!" Much to her chagrin, he leaped up and snapped the thongs easily. He had tricked her.

What did Samson think when he saw sandal straps tied around

him? "Love is blind," one could suppose. Delilah had him intoxicated, captivated, and bewitched. Soon this blindness would bring
worse blindness. But to him his lady love was playing an innocent
game. For her part, Delilah probably thought, *So he wants to play games,
eh? I'll show him how to play games!* With a wounded look and pouting,
she strolled up to her man, grabbed his great calloused hands in her
delicate little fingers, and impishly scolded him: "You have made a
fool of me; you lied to me." Then, running her fingers up his arms
and gently massaging his bulging muscles, she looked forgivingly into
his eyes and said, "Come now, tell me how you can be tied."

Samson still did not realize that his dainty little jewel was intent
on his destruction. He kept the game going, saying, "If anyone ties
me securely with new ropes that have never been used, I'll become
as weak as any other man." So Delilah got new ropes, and when
Samson was asleep, she tied him up with them. Again with men hidden in the room, she called, "Samson, the Philistines are upon you!"
But he leaped up and snapped the ropes as if they were nothing.

Delilah was persistent. Exuding all the charm she could muster,
she said sweetly, "Until now, you have been making a fool of me and
lying to me. Tell me how you can be tied."

Samson did not sense the danger of their little game. He could
not resist her charms. Strangle a lion? Yes. But overcome his blinding passion for Delilah? No. He should have run for his life, but looking around the room for a creative idea, he saw the loom and said, "If
you weave the seven braids of my head into the fabric on the loom
and tighten it with the pin, I'll become as weak as any other man."

So Delilah tenderly stroked Samson's hair until he fell asleep, and
then she proceeded to weave his braids into the warp of the fabric on
the loom and tighten it with the pin. The loom itself would have been
a primitive type with two upright posts fixed in the ground. When she
had his hair tightly woven, she cried out, "Samson, the Philistines are
upon you!"

He leaped up, this time pulling up fabric, loom, and all with his
hair. Foiled again! Still, Delilah's intuition told her she was getting
closer, and she was. While Samson thought he still had things under

control, he had let Delilah come perilously close to the truth. Cloaking her frustration, she drew him to the couch beside her and carefully began to untangle his hair.

With each loss, Delilah's tone of hurt and reproach increased. This time she took a powerful weapon from her arsenal. Looking truly wounded and distraught, she whined, "How can you say, 'I love you,' when you won't confide in me? This is the third time you have made a fool of me and haven't told me the secret of your great strength." She probably began to sob.

Evidently the Philistines had gone home at this point, figuring their tactic had failed. But the persuader extraordinaire was not finished. With heartless efficiency, she began wearing . . . wearing . . . wearing Samson down, nagging and prodding at him incessantly. She pestered him "day after day until he was tired to death." The fact that he kept loving her did nothing to soften her heart. Spurred on by visions of wealth and victory, she kept at him.

Perhaps considerable time had elapsed since Delilah's previous failures, but the ultimate effect of this tactic was devastating. She completely sapped him emotionally. He reached the point that he would do anything to stop her needling and wheedling, anything for a bit of peace. We can almost see him throwing his hands up in the air with an "I give up" gesture.

Samson told Delilah everything. "No razor has ever been used on my head," he confessed, "because I have been a Nazirite set apart to God since birth. If my head were shaved, my strength would leave me, and I would become as weak as any other man."

Gone was the twinkle in his eye, the playful look, the light-hearted reply. Delilah sensed defeat in his spirit as he soberly surrendered to her. This time she was certain he had betrayed his secret. And it made such sense! No one else had such long hair. Surely this head of hair *was* special. Cut it off and Samson's strength was *history*!

Cradling him, perhaps singing him sweet lullabies, she stroked her trusting lover to sleep on her lap. As she gently massaged his scalp and combed his hair with her fingers, he trusted her implicitly. He gratefully fell into a sound sleep.

With pulse-pounding certainty, wicked Delilah eased away from Samson and sent word to the Philistine rulers. "Come back once more," she said, "he has told me everything." So they came quickly, loaded with silver.

She let a barber into the room, who carefully began to lop off the sleeping man's hair, braid by braid. Then, the Bible says, Delilah "began to subdue him." Evidently, as before, she tied him up in some way to test his strength and shook him awake, crying again, "Samson, the Philistines are upon you!" Leaping up, he thought, *I'll go out as before and shake myself free.*

Recorded here, however, are some of the saddest words in the Bible: "But he did not know that the LORD had left him" (Judges 16:20). How tragic for one whose entire life had been dedicated to God, who enjoyed a mighty anointing of God's Spirit, not even to realize that the Spirit of God, his source of strength, had left him. He tried to free himself but could not. He had no strength!

When Delilah saw this, she called the Philistines into the room. They seized him and immediately gouged out his eyes so they would have the advantage if his strength returned. Never again would his eyes, the inlets of his sin, lead him to lose his senses over a woman.

As with Judas, who betrayed Jesus for thirty pieces of silver, this female Judas betrayed Israel's judge, by comparison winning a mother lode of silver. Mighty Samson, shorn of his strength, hung limp as a filleted fish as they carted him down to Gaza. They threw him in prison, put him in bronze shackles, and forced him to grind at the mill.

Samson's loss was not physical only. Satan had deceived him, blinding his spiritual eyes, plunging him into a dungeon of sin, and setting him grinding under its power. Not only did his physical enemies rejoice, but so did his spiritual ones. Now consigned to see nothing but the haunting memories of his failures, pictures of his lovely hoodwinker no doubt assaulted his mind constantly.

Sometime later Samson's hair began to grow—as did his repentance—and his strength started to return. One day the rulers of all the Philistines assembled at the temple of their god Dagon to celebrate

Samson's capture and to offer Dagon a great sacrifice. They cheered, "Our god has delivered Samson, our enemy, into our hands. . . . the one who laid waste our land and multiplied our slain." In high spirits they then shouted, "Bring out Samson to entertain us." Seeing him blind and fettered made them even more jubilant. They probably mocked, goaded, hit, and spat at him as he helplessly and heartbrokenly groped and stumbled about.

After a while they stood him among the temple's pillars where he got an idea. Feigning exhaustion, he asked the lad who led him by the hand to put him between two supporting pillars so he could rest against them. The temple was full of prominent people, including those who had bribed Delilah. On its flat roof another 3,000 people sat. Was Delilah home sipping on a mint julep, counting her cash, and enjoying her new life as a rich lady that day? Or was she in the crowd? It seems they might have invited the national heroine to a front-row seat along with the other dignitaries. If so, she had little time to enjoy her winnings.

She would see her former lover lift his face to heaven and quietly utter a prayer to his God. "O Sovereign LORD, remember me," he prayed. "O God, please strengthen me just once more, and let me with one blow get revenge on the Philistines for my two eyes." No one heard his words, but everyone saw him pray. A hush fell upon everyone as they watched him put each of his hands on a pillar. Suddenly his voice rang out, "Let me die with the Philistines!" He began to push. The temple quivered.

One can almost imagine Delilah jumping to her feet and screaming, "Samson, stop!" in hopes of soliciting his obedience one more time. But it was too late. A feminine voice would never again seduce him. The building collapsed with a thundering crash. Samson literally "brought the house down" that day. He died, but he took his enemies with him. The Bible says, "Thus he killed many more when he died than while he lived" (Judges 17:7-30).

Samson's name means "like the sun." He had many bright days as he judged Israel for twenty years. But Delilah lassoed this sun, pulling down its glory and forcing it to set behind a dark and stormy cloud. Still, despite his obvious weaknesses, he had a heart for God and ultimately plucked victory from the ashes for his God. Thus he made the roll of the New Testament's "Hall of Faith": "And what more shall I say? I do not have time to tell about Gideon, Barak, *Samson*, Jephthah, David, Samuel and the prophets, who through faith conquered kingdoms, administered justice, and gained what was promised; who shut the mouths of lions . . . whose weakness was turned to strength; and who became powerful in battle and routed foreign armies" (Hebrews 11:32-34).

We can find no positive word, however, for Samson's scheming lady love who, with honey on her lips and poison in her heart, manipulated him to annihilation for her personal gain.

## LESSONS FOR OUR OWN HEARTS

When Clay was a missionary in Berkeley many years ago, he accidentally stumbled through the door of a women's self-defense class. Suddenly a group of angry amazons came flying at him, letting him know that if he did not leave their turf by the count of "one," they would demonstrate their techniques on him. In his mind the only thing they lacked was combat fatigues. He bolted!

These women were training to subdue the enemy, i.e., the male species, combatively. Largely, however, women can never match men muscle for muscle. We might see some little woman chasing Hulk Hogan around the wrestling ring with a baseball bat, but I don't think anyone really buys it.

No, women have other tools, much more subtle yet effective, for their conquests. God gave us feminine charm and beauty as wonderful gifts. The God-designed attraction between males and females brings us together so we can complete each other. Unfortunately, however, sin corrupted God's intent. Since the Fall both sexes have used their innate strengths against each other, not to complete but to compete. The woman, whom God created as a suitable companion, a coworker, and a loving complement to man, has struck back against male domination by trying, in turn, to subdue him. Since she generally cannot dominate and control a man overtly, she often resorts to the much more subtle approach of manipulation.

---

*See, this alone I found, that God made human beings straightforward, but they have devised many schemes.*

ECCLESIASTES 7:29 NRSV

---

A fawning woman can quickly drive a brawny man to his knees. Just look at Delilah! The sirens of Greek mythology could not have done a better job of sweetly luring their male victims to shipwreck and death. For all of Samson's physical might, he was no match for Delilah. Doing what the Philistines had tried and failed to do for years, she quickly felled this muscle-bound Atlas of a man, giving him the world's worst "bad-hair day!" Captivated by her outward charm, he assumed that she was as beautiful inwardly. He mistook her sweet talk for love reciprocated. Sniffing deeply of her deceptive fragrance, he threw everything away for her love. Meanwhile, she went for the bag of money, putting no value at all on Samson's love, devotion, and loyalty to her—or even on his life.

What words can describe the cold-hearted, poisonous woman that would lull her man to sleep with his head in her lap, conscious of the terrible fate to which she would deliver him? What could be more wicked than a manipulative heart, treacherously using love to conquer and betray?

One can rarely find a male black widow spider. Want to know why? Because the sweet, little female lovingly holds her mate in her arms, saying, "I'm all yours, handsome." Their lovemaking, however, leaves him sleepy. And it leaves her hungry! She suddenly sees him in a new light and, casting love aside, kills and eats him. The poor guy never knew what hit him!

Okay, this is an extreme. Still, men have their weaknesses that make women's strengths all the more dangerous when pitted against them. The devil has taught many physically lovely yet poisonous women well in the craft of manipulation. For manipulation is his own greatest skill, without which he would have no power over God's people. He has no real advantage until we ignorantly fall to his manipulative schemes. He distorts our view of God, diverts us from spiritual realities, influences us to mistrust other Christians, enlists us to start church fights, moves us to isolate ourselves, convinces us to sin, provokes us to ruin our families. He does these and many other things through his deceptive manipulations. We must know that Satan is our coconspirator when we resort to manipulation to fulfill our purposes.

Clay was a young youth pastor when he stood in the pulpit delivering one of his first sermons. The message pertained to Satan's seductive devices and how to resist temptation. A luscious blonde from the youth group planted herself on the front row. As she seductively smiled and let her skirt rise way up her legs, no one could tell Clay the devil was not her coconspirator.

The devil, of course, incites men to manipulate women, too. But there is just no way of getting around it: Women catch on to the craft early. Just think of the cute, little girl on Daddy's lap, hugging him, loving him, making him feel like a god. What Mommy refused her, she will worm out of Daddy. Think about her heart. Sure, she loves her Daddy and wants to please him. But her sinful nature twists the beauty of their relationship by using it to her own ends. She is going to get all the mileage she can from her time on Daddy's lap. She has already mastered the art of manipulation.

When we give our lives to Christ, we come with habits like this that must be broken. Such behaviors are not becoming to a child of God. Now we have a new way of living and relating wherein we trust God to fill our needs. We no longer get what we want the same way we once did.

We may never have had a wickedly manipulative heart to Delilah's degree. Still, we should look well at our own subtle or not-so-subtle tendencies to deceive and manipulate. Before I became a Christian, I had lived a certain way in the world. I was never good at sweet-talking a man, but I was good at flirting with "come hither" looks. I always figured I had to "catch" the man of my dreams, and I used my feminine leverage to that end. I had a manipulative heart.

Then I became a Christian at the age of twenty-three. The Lord began to chip away at my manipulative devices. How can I forget the Sunday morning when I left for church with a middle-aged friend? She asked, "Is that really how you want to dress for church?" I looked down at my sexy attire, and a light went on. My heart no longer wanted those old ways. Wanting to please Jesus, I started to become aware of my tendencies and to change my ways. I cried, "I want a pure heart!"

Once I suddenly caught myself flirting with a church elder for whom I felt no attraction. I did not hear it in anything I said, but I felt it in my dancing eyes. It scared me. I thought that if I were flirting without even intending it, I must have a deep-seated problem. Realizing I had more than a habit to break, that I had a spiritual condition to renounce, I commanded that demonic seduction away from me. It left, never to return. Still, I have been tempted at times to manipulate situations for my own ends. To my knowledge, however, my heart has rarely let me act on such impulses.

Manipulation damages not only male/female relationships but church relationships as well. Some people, with gripes about their church or its leadership, deviously start backbiting and enlisting support for their positions. "Have you noticed how the church leaders try to run everything?" they ask. "Have you noticed that the pastor's preaching is not holding people's interest lately?" "Why, if they put me on the board, things sure would change." If these folks had any heart to resolve their complaints, they would go directly to the pastor rather than doing an end run around him. However, they prefer to maneuver quietly behind the scenes to get their way. Their listeners soon begin to pick up the same attitudes. Now this is not to say that things never need changing. The issue here is our hearts and how they lead us to go about seeking the changes.

How sad that people sometimes use their God-given gifts to manipulate others. They may have a preaching, teaching, prophetic, management, or other gift, and use it for manipulative purposes. I hate to say it, but this is a form of witchcraft. No, we are not talking about incantations, potions, and unsightly old hags here; we are talking about shrewdly using the power of manipulation to influence or manage people. Legitimate preaching, teaching, and prophecy that is God-inspired exhorts, encourages, and edifies, but never manipulates.

Let's look again at Abigail and Delilah. Both powerfully influenced their men; both had goals and a mission to accomplish. But they got what they wanted in opposite ways with opposite results because they had opposite hearts. Think about their differences:

Abigail had a good heart; Delilah had an evil heart.

Abigail used her persuasive gifts prudently; Delilah used her persuasive gifts manipulatively.

Abigail relied on godly wisdom to convince; Delilah relied on sensuality to conquer.

Abigail was honest and straightforward; Delilah was dishonest and scheming.

Abigail wisely rose to solve a crisis; Delilah wickedly sank to create one.

Abigail worked *for* everyone; Delilah greedily schemed *against* Samson.

Abigail appealed to David's highest nature to do the right thing; Delilah preyed upon Samson's lowest, basest nature to do a foolish thing.

Abigail dealt with David in a way that prevented him from carrying out a regrettable decision; Delilah led Samson to make the worst decision of his life, one he would regret till his dying breath.

Abigail won David's heart by sincerely building him up; Delilah won Samson's heart by insincerely manipulating him.

Abigail helped David remember who he was in God; Delilah made Samson forget who he was in God.

Abigail aided her nation; Delilah damaged it.

Abigail fulfilled God's purposes; Delilah opposed God's purposes.

Abigail brought light and life; Delilah brought blindness and death.

While Abigail managed people, Delilah manipulated them. Managing people without manipulating them is definitely a delicate art. But it is an important one, as we see. For us, it means knowing who we are in Christ and also respecting who others are in Christ.

Those with whom we are closest eventually reveal their weaknesses and vulnerabilities. We must never use this knowledge for manipulative purposes. That would mean repaying trust with deception. We should treasure, and never exploit, the love and trust given us, especially that of a husband. While we all have self-serving yearnings, we must choose the way that shows interest for the needs and feelings of others, that lays our own desires aside and does what is best for them.

If you somehow find yourself dissatisfied and want to see changes, you should remember the Holy Spirit's role. He is the ultimate change agent in your life and in the lives of others. If you pray and learn to trust God, He will replace any bad treasure in your heart with His good treasure; then you will be far less tempted to manipulate. Every time we manipulate others, we damage our own souls and lop off a braid of our victims' spiritual strength.

### Heart Check

1. In seeing the opposite fruit of Abigail's and Delilah's hearts, whose tactics for influencing people will you choose? Do you see manipulative tendencies that you need to renounce?

2. Can you remember times you have used your persuasive power to challenge others to be the best they can be? Can you remember times you have used this power to defeat others?

3. Have you ever cheated your man out of his spiritual calling? Have you ever used sex as a weapon against him?

4. What is the most important principle you can apply to your life from Delilah's example?

5. Compose a prayer in response to this chapter's lessons.

# NOTES

## Chapter 2: Jezebel

1. Ethbaal is the Hebrew translation meaning "man of Baal."
2. This account is recorded in 1 Kings 18.
3. This account is in 1 Kings 21.
4. See 2 Kings 9 for this account.

## Chapter 3: Rahab

1. Deuteronomy 34:3
2. See Nahshon in Exodus 6:23; Numbers 1:7; 2:3; 7:12,17; 10:14.
3. "Nahshon the father of Salmon, Salmon the father of Boaz, whose mother was Rahab, Boaz the father of Obed, whose mother was Ruth, Obed the father of Jesse, and Jesse the father of King David. . . . and Jacob the father of Joseph, the husband of Mary, of whom was born Jesus, who is called Christ" (Matthew 1:4-6, 16).

## Chapter 4: Eve

1. Rib (*telsa*, Heb.) literally means a "part of the side."
2. James 2:3

## Chapter 5: Ruth

1. Leviticus 19:9; 23:22; Deuteronomy 24:19
2. Deuteronomy 25:5-10
3. 2 Corinthians 8:21

## Chapter 6: Michal

1. 2 Samuel 6:23
2. Luke 5:36-39

## Chapter 7: Sarah

1. Genesis 36:31; 1 Chronicles 1:43
2. Revelation 1:6 (also 5:10) KJV
3. Nehemiah 9:8
4. Hebrews 11:14

5. 1 Peter 3:7

6. Genesis 12:14-15

7. Hammurabi was a king of ancient Mesopotamia known for putting the laws of his country into a formal code.

8. Genesis 24:67

9. Romans 4:11; Galatians 3:7

10. 1 Peter 3:4

11. 1 Peter 3:6

12. 1 John 4:19

## Chapter 8: Potiphar's Wife

1. This sequence of events is found in Genesis 37.

2. Genesis 39:1

## Chapter 9: Mary of Bethany

1. Matthew 8:20

2. From Matthew 21:17 and Mark 11:11 we see Jesus sometimes leaving Jerusalem to lodge in Bethany.

3. Variations of this story are told in Matthew 26:6-13, Mark 14:1-10, and John 12:1-8. While John presents the likeliest chronology, Matthew and Mark put it just before the Last Supper, perhaps to contrast Mary's total devotion with the indignant disciples, especially Judas whose ugly betrayal comes next.

4. Simon the Leper is the host in Matthew 26:6 and Mark 14:3, while John puts it at Mary and Martha's home.

5. John, as if to clarify the other two accounts, stresses that Mary is the woman involved (John 12:1-8).

6. John 12:5. Matthew and Mark record the disciples as complaining. John mentions Judas, perhaps because he was the most vehement.

7. Jeremiah 29:13

## Chapter 10: Lot's Wife

1. See Genesis 11:24-32.

2. See Genesis 12.

3. Deuteronomy 29:23

4. 2 Peter 2:7-8

5. See Genesis 14.

6. Genesis 13:12

7. Genesis 14:12

8.  Genesis 19:1
9.  2 Peter 2:7-8
10. See Genesis 18:16-33.
11. 2 Peter 2:7-8
12. 2 Corinthians 6:1
13. Matthew 13:22
14. Hebrews 11:10

## Chapter 11: Abigail

1.  1 Samuel 25:3
2.  1 Samuel 27:3; 1 Chronicles 3:1
3.  1 Samuel 23:13
4.  1 Samuel 13:14
5.  1 Samuel 25:36
6.  1 Samuel 25:38
7.  1 Samuel 16:18
8.  Romans 12:19-21
9.  2 Corinthians 6:14 (KJV)
10. 1 Peter 3:1

## Chapter 12: Delilah

1.  Judges 2:16
2.  One who demonstrated his consecration to God by vowing never to drink wine or cut his hair.
3.  This incident is found in Judges 16:1-3.
4.  Eleven hundred silver shekels  weighed nearly thirty pounds!
5.  Judges 17:10